SECOND EDITION

SUMMIT
English for Today's World

1

Joan Saslow • Allen Ascher

Pronunciation Booster by Bertha Chela-Flores

S0-AJC-669

ALWAYS LEARNING   PEARSON

Summit: English for Today's World 1, Second Edition

Copyright © 2012 by Pearson Education, Inc.
All rights reserved. No part of this publication may be reproduced, stored in a retrieval system, or transmitted in any form or by any means, electronic, mechanical, photocopying, recording, or otherwise, without the prior permission of the publisher.

Pearson Education, 10 Bank Street, White Plains, NY 10606

Staff credits: The people who made up the *Summit 1* Student's Book team—representing editorial, production, design, and manufacturing—are Rhea Banker, Aerin Csigay, Dave Dickey, Aliza Greenblatt, Caroline Kasterine, Mike Kemper, and Martin Yu.

Text composition: TSI Graphics
Text font: Palatino 11/13
Cover photograph: Shutterstock.com
Cover design: Elizabeth Carlson

Library of Congress Cataloging-in-Publication Data

Saslow, Joan M.
  Summit 1 : English for today's world / Joan Saslow, Allen Ascher ; pronunciation booster
  by Bertha Chela-Flores — 2nd ed.
    p. cm.
  ISBN 0-13-246716-X — ISBN 0-13-267995-7 1. English language—Textbooks for foreign speakers.
  2. English language—Rhetoric. I. Chela Flores, Bertha. II. Ascher, Allen. III. Title. IV. Title: Summit one.
PE1128.S2756 2012
428.2'4--dc23

                    2011023392

Photo credits: All original photography by David Mager. Page 3 David Zimmerman/Masterfile; p. 8 (top) Denis Scott/Corbis, (left to right) Shutterstock.com, RubberBall/SuperStock, Michael Newman/PhotoEdit, Imageshop-Zefa Visual Media UK Ltd/Alamy, Image100/SuperStock; p. 9 Hulton-Deutsch Collection/Corbis; p. 16 Neal Preston/Corbis; p. 17 Jo Hale/Getty Images; p. 18 (left) Image100/SuperStock, (middle) RubberBall/SuperStock, (right) age fotostock/SuperStock; p. 20 Archivo Iconografico, S.A. /Corbis; p. 21 (left) Lee Celano/Getty Images, (middle) Fox Photos/Getty Images, (right) Bret Thompsett/Alpha/Globe Photos; p. 22 Hemera Technologies/Alamy; p. 26 Shutterstock.com; p. 27 David Buffington/Getty Images; p. 28 (left to right) Stockbyte, Photomorgana/Corbis, LWA-Dann Tardif/Corbis, BananaStock/Robert Harding; p. 30 Mediacolor's/Alamy; p. 32 Shutterstock.com; p. 33 G. Bliss/Masterfile; p. 34 (left) Camera Press Digital/Retna Ltd., (right) www.newmansown.com; p. 38 (top left) Kaz Mori/Getty Images, (bottom left) Martin Harvey/Alamy, (middle) Reuters/Corbis, (top right) Historical Picture Archive/Corbis, (top right inset) www.englishcountrydancing.org, (bottom right) Picture Finders Ltd./eStock Photo; p. 39 (left to right) Thinkstock/Alamy, Stadium Studio/Alamy, Royalty-Free/Corbis, Royalty-Free/Corbis; p. 43 (A) Shutterstock.com, (B) Blend Images/Alamy, (C) RubberBall/SuperStock, (D) age fotostock/Medioimages, (E) Pierre Vauthey/Corbis; p. 44 (goatee) Emely/zefa/Corbis, (sideburns) Dennis Galante/Corbis, (buzz) Latin Focus.com, (bald) George Shelley/Corbis, (dyed) Brand X Pictures/Alamy, (long) Mike Powell/Getty Images, (braids) Royalty-Free/Corbis, (highlights) Stockbyte; p. 45 (top left to right) Mauro Fermariello/Photo Researchers, Inc., Stockbyte/Getty Images, Chuck Pefley/Alamy, Getty Images, Cindy Charles/PhotoEdit, (bottom left to right) Gideon Mendel/Corbis, Ariel Skelley/Corbis, Shutterstock.com; p. 46 Valentino Maria Chandoha/Corbis Sygma; p. 50 (top) Paul Chesley/National Geographic Image Collection, (bottom) Panoramic Images/Getty Images, (right) Stephanie Maze/Woodfin Camp and Associates; p. 51 (top) Will & Deni McIntyre/Corbis, (bottom) Randy M. Ury/Corbis; p. 52 Christian Zachariasen/Corbis; p. 54 (left to right) Catherine Ledner/Getty Images, Michael Prince/Corbis, age fotostock/Jack Hollingsworth, Roberto Stelzer/Getty Images; p. 56 AP/Wide World Photos; p. 58 (top) Danny Lehman/Corbis, (bottom) age fotostock/SuperStock; p. 62 Private Collection, Archives Charmet/ Bridgeman Art Library; p. 63 Shutterstock.com; p. 66 Ellen Senisi/ The Image Works; p. 67 (parrot) Shutterstock.com, (cat) Digital Vision Ltd./SuperStock, (pit bull) Julia Fishkin/Getty Images, (pug) Chris Carlson, (python) Shutterstock.com, (mouse) Chris Collins/Corbis; p. 70 (left) Shutterstock.com, (right) age fotostock/SuperStock, (bottom) John Cancalosi/naturepl.com; p. 74 (TV) Jimmy Dorantes/Latin Focus.com, (magazine) Image courtesy of The Advertising Archives, (blimp) Shotfile/Alamy, (billboards) Liu Liqun/Corbis, (radio) Joe Tree/Alamy; p. 75 (left) Imagination Photo Design, (middle) Imagination Photo Design, (right) Frank Siteman/Photolibrary; p. 76 Jon Arnold Images/Alamy; p. 77 (perfumes) Raymond Patrick/Getty Images, (chocolates) C Squared Studios/Getty Images, (watches) Shutterstock.com, (sunglasses) Darren Robb/Getty Images, (bags) Samsonite Corporation, (umbrellas) Samsonite Corporation; p. 78 (top left) Shutterstock.com, (top right) Royalty-Free/Corbis, (bottom left and right) Shutterstock.com; 82 Brand X Pictures/Alamy; p. 86 (top) (c)The New Yorker Collection 2004 Lee Lorenz from cartoonbank.com. All rights reserved, (bottom) Marty Bucella http://members.aol.com/mjbtoons/index.html; p. 87 David Young-Wolff/Alamy; p. 88 ER Productions/Corbis; p. 92 (top) Jonathan Smith/Lonely Planet Images, (bottom) Imageshop-Zefa Visual Media UK Ltd/Alamy; p. 94 (top) PCL/Alamy, (bottom) View Stock/Alamy; p. 95 (left) Keith Levit Photography/Photolibrary, (middle) age fotostock/Creatas, (right) age fotostock/BananaStock; p. 99 (top) Bettmann/Corbis, (left) AF archive/Alamy; WorldAtlas.com/GraphicMaps.com; p. 102 (left) John W. Hoopes, (right) Universtiy of Bologna; p. 103 (left) Richard T. Nowitz/Getty Images, (middle) Yann Arthus-Bertrand/Corbis, (right) David Hardy/Photo Researchers, Inc.; p. 104 Bettmann/Corbis, (inset) Hulton Archive/Getty Images; p. 105 Getty Images; p. 106 (top left) Reuters/Corbis, (top right) AP/Wide World Photos, (left) AF archive/Alamy; p. 110 (top left) Image courtesy of The Advertising Archives, (top right) Royalty-Free/Corbis, (middle left) Image courtesy of The Advertising Archives, (middle right) Image courtesy of The Advertising Archives, (bottom left) Peter Cade/Getty Images, (bottom right) Rob Van Petten/Getty Images; p. 112 (go) Royalty-Free/Corbis, (chess) Royalty-Free/Corbis, (video) Michael A. Keller/Corbis, (ping) Dreamstime.com, (embroidery) Paul A. Souders/Corbis, (wood) Jim Craigmyle/Masterfile, (crochet) John and Lisa Merrill/Corbis, (karate) Doug Blane/Flow With Your Breath/Alamy, (aerobics) Jose Luis Pelaez, Inc./Corbis, (yoga) Peter Griffith/Masterfile, (antiques) Paul Barton/Corbis, (rabbits) age fotostock/Max Messerli, (coins) Don Farrall/Getty Images; p. 113 (left) John Foxx/Alamy, (middle) Shutterstock.com, (right) Image100/Alamy; p. 115 Dorling Kindersley; p. 118 Chad Slattery/Getty Images; p. 119 (far left) Amy and Chuck Wiley/Wales/Photolibrary, (top left) Rick Doyle/Corbis, (top right) David Madison/Getty Images, (bottom left) Jakob Helbig/Getty Images, (bottom middle) Jess Stock/Getty Images, (bottom right) Joe McBride/Getty Images.

Illustration credits: Steve Attoe pp. 42, 52, 90, 111; Mark Collins pp. 40, 65, 98; Francois Escalmel pp. 75, 81, 116; Maria LaFrance, p. 10; Marc Mongeau p. 22; Dusan Petricic pp. 30, 101, 105, 118; Craig Spearing p. 68; Eve Steccati p. 104; Jean Wiesenbaugh p. 2.

ISBN 13 : 978-0-13-246716-2
ISBN 10 : 0-13-246716-X

1 2 3 4 5 6 7 8 9 10 – V042 – 16 15 14 13 12 11

ISBN 13 : 978-0-13-267986-2 (with MyEnglishLab)
ISBN 10 : 0-13-267986-8 (with MyEnglishLab)

1 2 3 4 5 6 7 8 9 10 – V042 – 16 15 14 13 12 11

Printed in the United States of America

About the Authors

Joan Saslow

Joan Saslow has taught in a variety of programs in South America and the United States. She is author of a number of multi-level integrated-skills courses for adults and young adults: *Ready to Go: Language, Lifeskills, and Civics; Workplace Plus: Living and Working in English;* and of *Literacy Plus.* She is also author of *English in Context: Reading Comprehension for Science and Technology.* Ms. Saslow was the series director of *True Colors* and *True Voices.* She has participated in the English Language Specialist Program in the U.S. Department of State's Bureau of Educational and Cultural Affairs. Ms. Saslow is coauthor, with Allen Ascher, of *Top Notch: English for Today's World.*

Allen Ascher

Allen Ascher has been a teacher and a teacher trainer in China and the United States and taught in the TESOL Certificate Program at the New School in New York. He was also academic director of the International English Language Institute at Hunter College. Mr. Ascher is author of the "Teaching Speaking" module of *Teacher Development Interactive,* an online multimedia teacher-training program, and of *Think about Editing: A Grammar Editing Guide for ESL.* Mr. Ascher is coauthor, with Ms. Saslow, of *Top Notch: English for Today's World.*

Both Ms. Saslow and Mr. Ascher are frequent and popular speakers at professional conferences and international gatherings of EFL and ESL teachers.

Authors' Acknowledgments

The authors are indebted to the following educators who contributed invaluable feedback and suggestions for the second edition of *Summit.*

Diana Alicia Ávila Martínez, CUEC Monterrey, Mexico • **Shannon Brown,** Nagoya University of Foreign Languages, Nagoya, Japan • **Maria Claudia Campos de Freitas,** Metalanguage, São Paulo, Brazil • **Isidro Castro Galván,** Instituto Teocalli, Monterrey, Mexico • **Jussara Costa e Silva,** Prize Language School, São Paulo, Brazil • **Jacqueline Díaz Esquivel,** PROULEX, Guadalajara, Mexico • **Erika Licia Esteves Silva,** Murphy English, São Paulo, Brazil • **Miguel Angel Guerrero Pozos,** PROULEX, Guadalajara, Mexico • **Cesar Guzmán,** CAADI Monterrey, Mexico • **César Iván Hernández Escobedo,** PROULEX, Guadalajara, Mexico • **Robert Hinton,** Nihon University, Tokyo, Japan • **Chandra Víctor Jacobs Sukahai,** Universidad de Valle de Mexico, Monterrey, Mexico • **Yeni Jiménez Torres,** Centro Colombo Americano Bogotá, Colombia • **Simon Lees,** Nagoya University of Foreign Languages, Nagoya, Japan • **Thomas LeViness,** PROULEX, Guadalajara, Mexico • **Amy Lewis,** Waseda University, Tokyo, Japan • **Tanja Maccandie,** Nagoya University of Foreign Languages, Nagoya, Japan • **Maria do Carmo Malavasi,** Avalon Language School, São Paulo, Brazil • **Tammy Martínez Nieves,** Universidad Autónoma de Nuevo León, Monterrey, Mexico • **Otilia Ojeda,** Monterrey, Mexico • **Henry Eduardo Pardo Lamprea,** Universidad Militar Nueva Granada, Colombia • **José Luis Pérez Treviño,** Instituto Obispado, Monterrey, Mexico • **Evelize** **Maria Placido Florian,** São Paulo, Brazil • **Armida Rivas,** Monterrey, Mexico • **Fabio Ossaamn Rok Kaku,** Prize Language School, São Paulo, Brazil • **Ana María Román Villareal,** CUEC, Monterrey, Mexico • **Peter Russell,** Waseda University, Tokyo, Japan • **Rubena St. Louis,** Universidad Simón Bolivar, Caracas, Venezuela • **Greg Strong,** Aoyama Gakuin University, Tokyo, Japan • **Gerry Talandis,** Toyo Gakuen University, Tokyo, Japan • **Stephen Thompson,** Nagoya University of Foreign Languages, Nagoya, Japan • **Ellen Yaegashi,** Kyoritsu Women's University, Tokyo, Japan • **Belkis Yanes,** Caracas, Venezuela • **Maria Cristina Zanon Costa,** Metalanguage, São Paulo, Brazil

Learning Objectives

Unit	Communication Goals	Vocabulary	Grammar
1 **New Perspectives** page 2	• Suggest ways to enjoy life more • Describe people's personalities • Compare perspectives on life • Share a life-changing experience	• Personality types **Word Skill:** • Classifying by positive and negative meaning	• Gerunds and infinitives: changes in meaning *GRAMMAR BOOSTER* • Gerunds and infinitives: summary • **Grammar for Writing:** parallelism with gerunds and infinitives
2 **Musical Moods** page 14	• Describe the music you listen to • Explain the role of music in your life • Describe a creative person • Discuss the benefits of music	• Elements of music • Describing creative personalities **Word Skill:** • Using participial adjectives	• The present perfect and the present perfect continuous: finished and unfinished actions • Noun clauses *GRAMMAR BOOSTER* • Finished and unfinished actions: summary • The past perfect continuous • **Grammar for Writing:** noun clauses as adjective and noun complements
3 **Money Matters** page 26	• Talk about your financial goals • Express buyer's remorse • Describe your spending habits • Discuss reasons for charitable giving	• Expressing buyer's remorse • Describing spending habits • Charity and investment	• Future plans and finished future actions • The past unreal conditional: inverted form *GRAMMAR BOOSTER* • The future continuous • The future perfect continuous
4 **Looking Good** page 38	• Discuss appropriate dress • Comment on fashion and style • Evaluate ways to change one's appearance • Discuss appearance and self-esteem	• Describing fashion and style **Word Skill:** • Using the prefix <u>self-</u>	• Quantifiers *GRAMMAR BOOSTER* • Quantifiers: review ○ <u>A few</u> and <u>few</u>, <u>a little</u> and <u>little</u> ○ Using <u>of</u> ○ Without referents • **Grammar for Writing:** subject-verb agreement with quantifiers with <u>of</u>
5 **Community** page 50	• Politely ask someone not to do something • Complain about public conduct • Discuss social responsibility • Identify urban problems	• Ways to soften an objection • Ways to perform community service **Word Skill:** • Using negative prefixes to form antonyms	• Possessives with gerunds • Paired conjunctions *GRAMMAR BOOSTER* • Conjunctions with <u>so</u>, <u>too</u>, <u>neither</u>, or <u>not either</u> • <u>So</u>, <u>too</u>, <u>neither</u>, or <u>not either</u>: short responses

Conversation Strategies	Listening/ Pronunciation	Reading	Writing
• Use <u>Actually</u> to soften a negative response • Use <u>I wonder</u> to elicit an opinion politely • Use <u>You know</u> to indicate that you are about to offer advice or a suggestion	**Listening Skills:** • Infer point of view • Listen for main ideas • Understand from context *PRONUNCIATION BOOSTER* • Content words and function words	**Texts:** • A magazine article about finding balance in life • A magazine article about optimism vs. pessimism • A survey about perspectives on life **Skills/strategies:** • Relate to personal experience • Identify supporting details	**Task:** • Describe personality types **Writing Skill:** • Paragraph structure: review
• Use <u>So</u> to indicate a desire to begin a conversation • Confirm information with <u>right?</u> • Use <u>You know</u> to introduce information and be less abrupt • Begin answers with <u>Well</u> to introduce an opinion	**Listening Skills:** • Listen to activate vocabulary • Listen for main ideas • Listen for supporting details *PRONUNCIATION BOOSTER* • Intonation patterns	**Texts:** • Brief CD reviews from a website • Interviews: the role of music in one's life • A biography of Ludwig van Beethoven **Skills/strategies:** • Make personal comparisons • Activate language from a text	**Task:** • Describe yourself **Writing Skill:** • Parallel structure
• Use <u>Hey</u> to indicate enthusiasm • Use <u>to tell you the truth</u> to introduce an unexpected assertion • Ask <u>What do you mean?</u> to clarify • Agree informally with <u>You're telling me</u>	**Listening Skills:** • Infer reasons • Listen for main ideas • Listen for details *PRONUNCIATION BOOSTER* • Sentence rhythm	**Texts:** • Financial tips from a newspaper • Interviews: financial goals • A magazine article about Paul Newman's philanthropy **Skills/strategies:** • Make personal comparisons • Express and support an opinion	**Task:** • Explain your financial goals **Writing Skill:** • Sequencing events: review
• Use <u>Can you believe</u> to indicate disapproval • Use <u>Don't you think</u> to promote consensus • Begin a response with <u>Well</u> to convey polite disagreement or reservation • Stress the main verb to acknowledge only partial agreement	**Listening Skills:** • Infer information • Listen to activate vocabulary • Listen to summarize • Express and support an opinion *PRONUNCIATION BOOSTER* • Linking sounds	**Texts:** • A newspaper article about casual dress at work • A magazine article about how the media affects self-image **Skills/strategies:** • Examine cultural expectations • Identify supporting details • Apply ideas	**Task:** • Compare two people's tastes in fashion **Writing Skill:** • Compare and contrast: review
• Use <u>Do you mind</u> to express concern that an intended action may offend • Use <u>Actually</u> to object politely • Use expressions such as <u>I hope that's not a problem</u> to soften an objection • Say <u>Not at all</u> to indicate a willingness to comply	**Listening Skills:** • Listen to summarize • Listen for details • Critical thinking *PRONUNCIATION BOOSTER* • Unstressed syllables	**Texts:** • A graph depicting world population changes • Interviews: pet peeves about public conduct • An interview about "megacities" **Skills/strategies:** • Interpret data from a graph • Express your ideas • Confirm content • Understand from context • Infer information	**Task:** • Complain about a problem **Writing Skill:** • Formal letters: review

Unit	Communication Goals	Vocabulary	Grammar
6 **Animals** page 62	• Exchange opinions about the treatment of animals • Discuss the benefits of certain pets • Compare animal characters • Debate the value of animal conservation	• Ways animals are used or treated • Describing pets • Describing character traits	• The passive voice with modals *GRAMMAR BOOSTER* • Modals and modal-like expressions: summary
7 **Advertising and Consumers** page 74	• Give shopping advice • Discuss your reactions to ads • Persuade someone to buy a product • Describe consumer shopping habits	• Describing low prices and high prices • Shopping expressions • Ways to persuade	• Passive forms of gerunds and infinitives *GRAMMAR BOOSTER* • **Grammar for Writing:** past forms of gerunds and infinitives
8 **Family Trends** page 86	• Describe family trends • Discuss parent / teen issues • Compare generations • Describe care for the elderly	• Examples of bad behavior • Describing parent and teen behavior **Word Skill:** • Transforming verbs and adjectives into nouns	• Repeated comparatives and double comparatives *GRAMMAR BOOSTER* • Making comparisons: summary • Other uses of comparatives, superlatives, and comparisons with <u>as</u> . . . <u>as</u>
9 **History's Mysteries** page 98	• Speculate about the out-of-the-ordinary • Present a theory about a past event • Discuss how believable a story is • Evaluate the trustworthiness of news sources	• Ways to say "I don't know" • Ways to express certainty **Word Skill:** • Using adjectives with the suffix <u>-able</u>	• Indirect speech with modals • Perfect modals in the passive voice for speculating about the past *GRAMMAR BOOSTER* • <u>Say</u>, <u>ask</u>, and <u>tell</u>: summary • **Grammar for Writing:** other reporting verbs
10 **Your Free Time** page 110	• Explain the benefits of leisure activities • Describe hobbies and other interests • Compare your use of leisure time • Discuss the risk-taking personality	• Ways to express fear and fearlessness **Word Skills:** • Using collocations for leisure activities • Modifying with adverbs	• Order of modifiers *GRAMMAR BOOSTER* • Adverbs of manner • Intensifiers

Pronunciation table / Irregular verbs .... page A2
Stative verbs / Verbs followed by a gerund / Expressions that can be followed by a gerund .... page A3
Verbs followed directly by an infinitive / Verbs followed by an object before an infinitive .... page A4
Adjectives followed by an infinitive .... page A4

Conversation Strategies	Listening/ Pronunciation	Reading	Writing
• Use <u>I've heard</u> to introduce a statement of popular opinion • Use <u>for one thing</u> to provide one reason among several in supporting an argument • Use <u>believe it or not</u> to introduce surprising information	**Listening Skills**: • Listen to activate vocabulary • Express and support an opinion • Draw conclusions • Make comparisons *PRONUNCIATION BOOSTER* • Sound reduction	**Texts:** • The Chinese Zodiac • A discussion board about the humane treatment of animals • An article about animal conservation **Skills/strategies:** • Evaluate ideas • Understand from context • Critical thinking	**Task:** • Express an opinion on animal treatment **Writing Skill:** • Persuasion
• Soften a wish or a statement of intent with <u>I think I'd like to</u> • Respond with <u>nothing in particular</u> to indicate indecision or avoid commitment • Make a suggestion by saying something <u>would be a good bet</u> • Say <u>Of course</u> to make an affirmative answer stronger	**Listening Skills**: • Listen to activate vocabulary • Support reasoning with details • Apply ideas *PRONUNCIATION BOOSTER* • Vowel sounds	**Texts:** • Interviews: reactions to ads • A presentation of eight advertising techniques • A magazine article about compulsive shopping **Skills/strategies:** • Understand from context • Infer information • Relate to personal experience	**Task:** • Explain an article you read **Writing Skill:** • Summarize and paraphrase another person's ideas
• Use <u>I hate to say it, but</u> to introduce unwelcome information • Respond with <u>I suppose</u> to indicate partial agreement • Use <u>But</u> to introduce a dissenting opinion	**Listening Skills**: • Listen to apply grammar • Listen to activate vocabulary • Make personal comparisons • Listen to summarize • Listen for details • Compare and contrast • Critical thinking *PRONUNCIATION BOOSTER* • Stress placement	**Texts:** • A brochure about falling birthrates • A newspaper article about China's elderly population • Case studies: aging parents **Skills/strategies:** • Identify cause and effect • Summarize • Confirm content • Draw conclusions	**Task:** • Describe your relationship with a family member **Writing Skill:** • Avoiding run-on sentences and comma splices
• Respond with <u>Beats me</u> to admit lack of knowledge • Say <u>You're probably right</u> to acknowledge another's encouragement • Ask a question with <u>Why else would</u> to confirm one's own opinion	**Listening Skills**: • Listen for main ideas • Listen to summarize • Draw conclusions *PRONUNCIATION BOOSTER* • Reduction and linking	**Texts:** • Encyclopedia entries about well-known mysteries • A magazine article about the world's greatest hoaxes **Skills/strategies:** • Draw conclusions • Activate prior knowledge • Confirm facts	**Task:** • Write a news article **Writing Skill:** • Avoiding sentence fragments
• Use <u>kind of like</u> to make a loose comparison • Use <u>I hate to say this, but</u> to excuse oneself for disagreeing • Use <u>Well, even so</u> to acknowledge someone's point but disagree politely	**Listening Skills**: • Listen to define • Relate to personal experience *PRONUNCIATION BOOSTER* • Vowel sounds	**Texts:** • Statistics comparing technological promises vs. reality • Message-board posts about unusual hobbies • A magazine article about technology and leisure time **Skills/strategies:** • Draw conclusions • Identify supporting details	**Task:** • Comment on another's point of view **Writing Skill:** • Expressing and supporting opinions clearly

Verbs that can be followed by a gerund or an infinitive / Participial adjectives .... page A4
Grammar Booster .... page G1
Pronunciation Booster .... page P1

What is *Summit*?

Summit is a two-level* high-intermediate to advanced communicative course for adults and young adults that can follow any intermediate-level course book.

The goal of the *Summit* course is to make English unforgettable, enabling post-intermediate learners to understand, speak, read, and write English accurately, confidently, and fluently through:

► Multiple exposures to new language
► Numerous opportunities to practice it
► Deliberate and intensive recycling

Each full level of *Summit* contains enough material for 60 to 90 hours of classroom instruction. Alternatively, *Summit* Student's Books are available in split editions with bound-in Workbooks. A wide choice of supplementary components makes it easy to tailor *Summit* to the needs of your classes.

Summit is designed to follow the *Top Notch* series, forming the top two levels of a complete six-level course.

The *Summit* Instructional Design

Balanced development of fluency and accuracy

Every two-page lesson culminates in a free discussion, debate, presentation, role play, or project. Planning activities such as idea framing and notepadding lead students to confident spoken expression in those activities. Grammar is tightly integrated with the speaking syllabus for memorability. Grammar charts include clear rules, examples, and explanations of meaning and use. Authentic readings further reinforce target grammar in natural contexts.

Essential conversation models for post-intermediate students

Because post-intermediate students continue to need intensive development of spoken communication, *Summit* provides ten essential conversation models that embed crucial conversation strategies and provide a starting point for personalized communication. Subsequent free communication activities are crafted so students can continually retrieve and use the language from the models. All conversation models are informed by the Longman Corpus of Spoken American English.

Academic skills and strategies

Each unit in the *Summit* course contains exercises that build key reading, listening, and critical thinking skills and strategies, such as paraphrasing, drawing conclusions, expressing and supporting an opinion, and activating prior knowledge. These exercises develop analytical skills while providing additional opportunities for learners to support their answers through speaking.

A high-impact vocabulary syllabus

Vocabulary in *Summit* is presented at word, phrase, and sentence levels, and includes expressions, idioms, and collocations. A concurrent emphasis on word skills enables students to expand their vocabulary by learning word transformation, classification, association, and other skills. Word skills practice increases students' mastery in both comprehending and producing new vocabulary.

A writing syllabus dedicated to the conventions of written English

Summit teaches the conventions of English writing so students will be prepared for standardized tests as well as further academic study. Key writing and rhetorical skills such as using parallel structure, avoiding sentence fragments, expressing and supporting an opinion, and persuading the reader are clearly presented and applied in carefully structured writing tasks. Additional *Grammar for Writing* sections build further awareness of these conventions.

ActiveBook

SECOND EDITION

SUMMIT
with ActiveBook
1

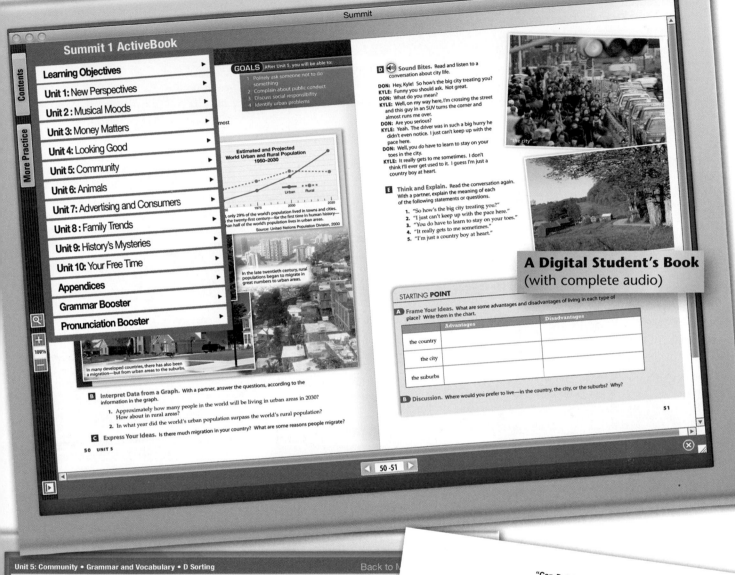

Summit 1 ActiveBook

Learning Objectives

- Unit 1: New Perspectives
- Unit 2: Musical Moods
- Unit 3: Money Matters
- Unit 4: Looking Good
- Unit 5: Community
- Unit 6: Animals
- Unit 7: Advertising and Consumers
- Unit 8: Family Trends
- Unit 9: History's Mysteries
- Unit 10: Your Free Time
- Appendices
- Grammar Booster
- Pronunciation Booster

Contents · **More Practice**

GOALS After Unit 5, you will be able to:
1 Politely ask someone not to do something
2 Complain about public conduct
3 Discuss social responsibility
4 Identify urban problems

Estimated and Projected World Urban and Rural Population 1950–2030

Urban   Rural

Source: United Nations Population Division, 2000

In the late twentieth century, rural populations began to migrate in great numbers to urban areas.

In many developed countries, there has also been a migration—but from urban areas to the suburbs.

B Interpret Data from a Graph. With a partner, answer the questions, according to the information in the graph.
1. Approximately how many people in the world will be living in urban areas in 2030? How about in rural areas?
2. In what year did the world's urban population surpass the world's rural population?

C Express Your Ideas. Is there much migration in your country? What are some reasons people migrate?

50   UNIT 5

D Sound Bites. Read and listen to a conversation about city life.

DON: Hey, Kyle! So how's the big city treating you?
KYLE: Funny you should ask. Not great.
DON: What do you mean?
KYLE: Well, on my way here, I'm crossing the street and this guy in an SUV turns the corner and almost runs me over.
DON: Are you serious?
KYLE: Yeah. The driver was in such a big hurry he didn't even notice. I just can't keep up with the pace here.
DON: Well, you do have to learn to stay on your toes in the city.
KYLE: It really gets to me sometimes. I don't think I'll ever get used to it. I guess I'm just a country boy at heart.

"the city"

E Think and Explain. Read the conversation again. With a partner, explain the meaning of each of the following statements or questions.
1. "So how's the big city treating you?"
2. "I just can't keep up with the pace here."
3. "You do have to learn to stay on your toes."
4. "It really gets to me sometimes."
5. "I'm just a country boy at heart."

A Digital Student's Book
(with complete audio)

STARTING POINT

A Frame Your Ideas. What are some advantages and disadvantages of living in each type of place? Write them in the chart.

	Advantages	Disadvantages
the country		
the city		
the suburbs		

B Discussion. Where would you prefer to live—in the country, the city, or the suburbs? Why?

51

50 -51

Unit 5: Community • Grammar and Vocabulary • D Sorting   Back to M

Drag each adjective into the negative prefix it uses.

courteous | rational | responsible | proper | imaginable | honest | acceptable | excusable | respectful | polite
appropriate | pleasant | considerate | mature

dis-	im-	in-	ir-	un-

Interactive practice (with daily activity records)
- ▶ Extra listening and reading comprehension
- ▶ Record-yourself speaking
- ▶ Grammar and vocabulary practice
- ▶ Games and puzzles

"Can-Do" Self-Assessment Chart
(Unit 5)

This chart will help you evaluate your own progress and identify language you may want to spend more time studying and practicing. After you have completed the unit, complete the chart below.

Evaluate your confidence about each "Can-Do" statement in the following. Check "1" if you feel very confident in your ability to use the language ... Check "3" if you are ... confident. Check "3" if you ... place in the unit where the ...

Self-assessment at the end of every unit

	Can-Do Sta...	Pages	1	2	3
Grammar	I can use pos... with gerunds.		☐	☐	☐
	I can contrast alternatives using paired conjunctions.	52	☐	☐	☐
Vocabulary	I can soften an objection in different ways.	54, 55	☐	☐	☐
	I can form antonyms using negative prefixes.	52	☐	☐	☐
Reading	I can describe different ways to perform community service.	53	☐	☐	☐
	I can interpret data from a graph.	56	☐	☐	☐
	I can understand a conversation about city life.	50	☐	☐	☐
	I can read postings about annoying behaviors.	51	☐	☐	☐
Listening	I can read an interview about Megacities.	54	☐	☐	☐
	I can understand a story about organ donation.	58	☐	☐	☐
	I can understand a narration of a series of events.	56	☐	☐	☐
Speaking	I can understand a conversation about cities.	56	☐	☐	☐
	I can see pictures and a graph to comment on changes in rural / urban populations.	61	☐	☐	☐
	I can frame and express my ideas about life in cities, suburbs, and the country.	50	☐	☐	☐
	I can role-play a conversation asking for permission to do something.	51	☐	☐	☐
	I can politely ask someone not to do someth...	52	☐	☐	☐
	I can use notes to ...				

Summit

The Teacher's Edition and Lesson Planner

Includes:
- ▶ A bound-in Methods Handbook for professional development
- ▶ Detailed lesson plans with suggested teaching times
- ▶ Language, culture, and corpus notes
- ▶ Student's Book and Workbook answer keys
- ▶ Audioscripts
- ▶ *Summit TV* teaching notes

▶ ActiveTeach

- ▶ A Digital Student's Book with interactive whiteboard (IWB) software
- ▶ Instantly accessible audio and *Summit TV* video
- ▶ Interactive exercises from the Student's *ActiveBook* for in-class use
- ▶ A complete menu of printable extension activities

Teacher's Edition and Lesson Planner with ActiveTeach
SECOND EDITION
SUMMIT 1
Joan Saslow • Allen Ascher
PEARSON

Summit TV
Authentic TV news documentaries and unrehearsed on-the-street interviews

The Digital Student's Book
With zoom, write, highlight, save and other IWB tools.

Printable Extension Activities
Including:
- • Discourse strategies
- • Extra writing skills practice
- • Reading strategies
- • Graphic organizers
- • Pronunciation activities
- • Video activity worksheets and more . . .

Discourse Strategies
(Unit 10, page 119)

Showing interest and surprise with short-form questions and statements

A. Use these short "tag"-like questions and statements to show interest and encourage further discussion. Practice saying each.

To show interest	To show surprise	To show strong surprise
use short-form questions with rising intonation	use emphatic questions with rising intonation	use negative statements with falling intonation
IS It? DID you? WERE they? WOULD he?	They DID? It HAD? They COULDn't?	You HADn'tl It DID'ntl She WASn'tl

B. Pair Work. Take turns reading the prompts below and using short-form questions and statements to show interest and surprise.

Student A begins

A: I was out late last night and the streets were deserted.
B: (Show interest.)
A: Yeah, it was strange!

A: My brother would always go skiing.
B: (Show interest.)
A: Yes, there was a ski resort nearby.

A: The rest of the group couldn't hear my shouts!
B: (Show surprise.)
A: No! I didn't know what to do!

A: And the bungee cord had started to tear!
B: (Show surprise.)

Student B begins

B: I went snorkeling in the Gulf of Mexico.
A: (Show interest.)
B: Yeah, it was great—beautiful fish.

B: It's a popular place for surfers in Hawaii.
A: (Show interest.)
B: Yeah, the waves can be very exciting.

B: And the crabs started crawling over my sleeping bag.
A: (Show surprise.)
B: Yeah, it was scary.

B: She was falling off the edge of the cliff!
A: (Show strong surprise.)
B: Yes, she was!

NAME: _____ DATE: _____

Extra Writing Skills Practice
(Unit 10, page 120)

Expressing and Supporting Opinions Clearly

A. Circle the best connecting word or phrase in each set.

Jon Katz says that cell phones make us feel more stress... Because of) cell phones, most people feel more relaxed. (● Due... of cell phones, you can easily call family and friends to let them... (● In addition / Since), if you are looking for a friend in a crowd... you need to do is call your friend on your cell phone. (● Becaus... always use the cell phone to get directions. (● Finally / This is w... situation, you can call for help right away. Cell phones definitel...

B. Fill in the blanks with one of the connecting words or phrases... (Two phrases will not be used.)

- • in addition
- • due to
- • first of all
- • also
- • this is why
- • finally

The author says, "The technological tools we use to n... leisure time." I definitely agree with him in the case of cell pho...

● _____ people at work think they can call m... and even on the weekends. ● _____, m... work to solve any little problem that comes up. And my husb... with his problems—he's even worse than the kids are. ●...

NAME: _____

Reading Strategies
(Unit 6, page 70)

Guessing meaning from context

Learn to use the context of a reading to determine possible meanings of unfamiliar words.

Practice. Look at the highlighted words in context and choose the best definition for each. Explain your answers.

1. "The earth is rich in **biodiversity** with millions of different species of plants and animals."
   biodiversity
   a. endangered animals   b. the variety of living things   c. threats to nature

2. "...the giant panda's **habitat** has been **decimated**—the old-growth bamboo forests where the pandas make their home are being destroyed rapidly... (T)he polar bear's icy **habitat** is disappearing as a result of global warming, and it's survival is at risk."
   habitat
   a. the food animals eat   b. the place animals live   c. the extinction of animals
   decimated
   a. helped   b. destroyed   c. enlarged

3. "**Extinction** is one environmental problem that is truly irreversible—once gone, these species cannot be brought back."
   extinction
   a. global warming   b. trying to protect animals   c. the disappearance of a species

4. "...WWF has advanced giant panda **conservation** by training more than 300 panda reserve staff and local government officials, working with the community to help save habitat and guard against illegal hunting."
   conservation
   a. trying to protect animals   b. danger to animals   c. feeding animals

Other components

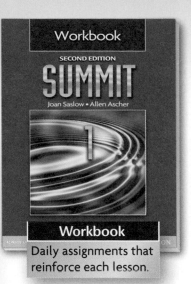

Workbook

Daily assignments that reinforce each lesson.

Classroom Audio Program

Includes a variety of authentic regional and non-native accents.

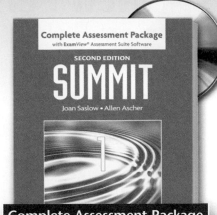

Complete Assessment Package

Ready-made achievement tests. Software provides option to edit, delete, or add items.

Full-Course Placement Tests

Four test forms to choose from.

MyEnglishLab

An optional online learning tool with:

► An interactive *Summit* Workbook
► Speaking and writing activities
► Pop-up grammar help
► Student's Book *Grammar Booster* and *Pronunciation Booster* exercises
► *Summit TV* with extensive viewing activities
► Automatically-graded achievement tests
► Easy course management and record-keeping

New Perspectives

GOALS After Unit 1, you will be able to:

1 Suggest ways to enjoy life more
2 Describe people's personalities
3 Compare perspectives on life
4 Share a life-changing experience

A **Topic Preview.** Look at the map of the world. Where do you think the artist is from?

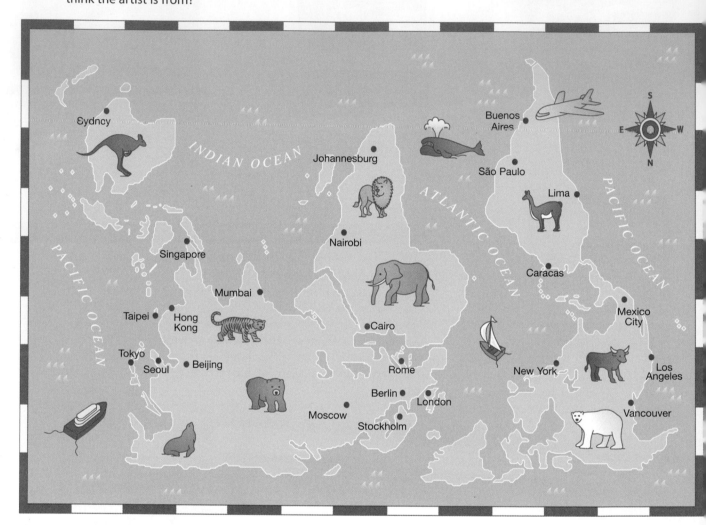

B **Express Your Ideas.**

1. What is unusual about the way the map depicts the world?

2. What do you think the artist is trying to say with the illustration? Is the artist being serious or funny?

C 🎧 1:02 **Sound Bites.** Read and listen to a conversation between two colleagues working temporarily in another country.

GILBERT: Oh, man! Am I ready to head home!

ANNA: Are you kidding? I can't get enough of this place.

GILBERT: Well, it's been three weeks, and I think I've had about enough. I'm tired of eating strange food.

ANNA: Wow! I feel just the opposite. I can't get over how much I enjoy being here. I love how different the food is.

GILBERT: Well, not me. And frankly, it's a pain in the neck having to work so hard to understand what people are saying to me.

ANNA: I actually think it's fun trying to figure out how to communicate. Stop complaining! You'll be home before you know it!

GILBERT: Fine by me. There's no place like home.

D **Think and Explain.** Read the conversation again. With a partner, explain the meaning of each of the following statements.

1. "Am I ready to head home!"
2. "I can't get enough of this place."
3. "I think I've had about enough."
4. "I can't get over how much I enjoy being here."
5. "It's a pain in the neck having to work so hard."
6. "There's no place like home."

E **Identify Supporting Details.** Read each statement and with a partner decide who you think said it—Anna or Gilbert. Support your opinion with information from the conversation.

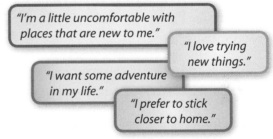

"I'm a little uncomfortable with places that are new to me."

"I love trying new things."

"I want some adventure in my life."

"I prefer to stick closer to home."

F **Compare and Contrast.** Discuss the questions.

1. How would you describe Anna's and Gilbert's personalities? How are they different?
2. Who are *you* more like, Gilbert or Anna?

STARTING **POINT**

Activate Language from a Text. Check which of the following statements you think you would make about foreign travel. Then compare and discuss opinions with a partner.

- ☐ "I can't get enough of visiting new and interesting places."
- ☐ "I love how different the food is."
- ☐ "It's a pain in the neck having to figure out what people are saying."
- ☐ "I think it's fun trying to figure out how to communicate when I don't know the language."
- ☐ "After a few days I'm ready to head home."
- ☐ Other: _____ .

3

1

GOAL
Suggest ways to enjoy life more

A 🎧 1:03 **Grammar Snapshot.** Read the article and notice the use of <u>forget</u>, <u>stop</u>, and <u>remember</u>.

Finding Balance

Are you burning the candle at both ends? Do you feel you have no time for yourself? Do you **forget to call** family on birthdays or holidays? Have you **stopped going out** with friends because you're too busy? Do you have trouble relaxing and having fun?

If you recognize yourself, you should **remember to slow down** and **take** more time for everything. Living a balanced life is about integrating the many vital areas of your life, including your health, friends, family, work, and romance.

Here are some tips for restoring a healthy perspective. First, **remember to make** time for the important people in your life. **Stop over-scheduling** and spend quality time with friends and family. Second, learn to eat, talk, walk, and drive more slowly. And **don't forget to turn** your cell phone **off** sometimes. People who really want to talk to you will call back. Third, learn to live in the present and **stop worrying** about the future. And finally, take it easy and begin enjoying the simple things in life. **Stop to smell** the roses.

B **Relate to Personal Experience.** Discuss the questions.

1. Did you recognize yourself or someone you know in the article? Give examples.
2. Did you find the tips helpful? Why or why not?

C Grammar. Gerunds and infinitives: changes in meaning

Some verbs are followed by either a gerund or an infinitive with no change in meaning,
for example: <u>love</u>, <u>hate</u>, <u>can't stand</u>, <u>like</u>, <u>prefer</u>, <u>begin</u>, <u>start</u>, <u>continue</u>.

Begin enjoying the simple things in life. OR **Begin to enjoy** the simple things in life.

Some verbs change meaning, depending on whether they are followed by a gerund or an infinitive.

<u>remember</u> + infinitive = remember to do something
Remember to make time for the important people in your life.
I have to **remember to send** an e-mail to my friend.

<u>remember</u> + gerund = remember something that happened in the past
I **remember having** more time for myself.
Do you **remember going** there when you were a kid?

<u>forget</u> + infinitive = forget to do something
Don't forget to turn your cell phone off.
He always **forgets to call** on my birthday.

<u>forget</u> + gerund = forget something that happened in the past
I'll never **forget seeing** the mountains for the first time.
Can you ever **forget going** to the beach?

<u>stop</u> + infinitive = stop in order to do something
Stop to smell the roses.
Can you **stop to pick up** some chocolates for the party?

<u>stop</u> + gerund = stop an ongoing action
Stop over-scheduling and spend quality time with friends and family.
You need to **stop worrying** so much.

REMEMBER

Some verbs are followed by infinitives.
Learn to live in the present.

Some verbs are followed by gerunds.
I **enjoy spending** time with my friends.

Some verbs are followed by objects
and infinitives.
He **reminded me to call** my mother.

For a complete list of verbs followed
by gerunds, infinitives, and objects
and infinitives, see page A3 in the
Appendices.

GRAMMAR BOOSTER
▸ p. G1
• Gerunds and infinitives:
summary
• Parallelism with gerunds
and infinitives

D Grammar Practice. Complete each sentence with a gerund or an infinitive.
Explain the meaning of each sentence.

*"Number 1 is about remembering
something that happened in the past."*

1. I'll never forget (travel) .... abroad for the first time.

2. When I feel stressed out, I remember (put) .... things in
   perspective.

3. You need to stop (try) .... to do everything at once.

4. If I forget (send) .... a card for a friend's birthday, I try to remember (call) ....

5. We forgot (buy) .... flowers, so we stopped (pick up) .... some on the way to the party.

6. I remember (celebrate) .... holidays with my family when I was young.

NOW YOU CAN *Suggest ways to enjoy life more*

A **Notepadding.** With a partner, write a list of
suggestions for what someone can do to enjoy
life more. Use <u>remember</u>, <u>forget</u>, and <u>stop</u>.

Stop worrying about the small things.

B **Use the Grammar.** Share your ideas with
your class or group. Using the information on
your notepad, create a list of suggestions that
everyone agrees with.

2 GOAL
Describe people's personalities

A 🎧 1:04 **Conversation Snapshot.** Read and listen. Notice the conversation strategies.

A: Have you had a chance to meet the new manager?

B: Liz? **Actually**, no. Have you?

A: Not yet. **I wonder** what she's like.

B: Well, everyone says she's bad news.

A: **You know**, you can't believe everything you hear. She might turn out to be a real sweetheart.

🎧 1:05 **Rhythm and intonation practice**

B 🎧 1:06 **Vocabulary. Personality Types.** Listen and practice.

Positive
a sweetheart someone who is likable and easy to get along with
a team player someone who works well with other people so the whole group is successful
a brain someone who is intelligent and can solve problems that are difficult for others
a people person someone who likes being with and works well with other people

Negative
a tyrant someone, especially a boss, who makes people work extremely hard
a workaholic someone who is always working and does not have time for anything else
a pain in the neck someone who complains a lot and often causes problems
a wise guy someone who says or does annoying things, especially to make himself or herself seem smarter than other people

> **PRONUNCIATION BOOSTER** ▶ p. P1
> • Content words and function words

C 🎧 1:07 **Listening. Infer Point of View.** Listen carefully to the conversations about people's personalities. Infer which expression from the Vocabulary the speaker would use to describe the person.

1. The woman thinks that Shelly is ....
  a. a sweetheart   **b.** a brain   **c.** a pain in the neck

2. The woman thinks that Peter is ....
  a. a workaholic   **b.** a tyrant   **c.** a team player

3. The man thinks that Paul is ....
  a. a team player   **b.** a people person   **c.** a wise guy

D **Word Skills. Classifying by Positive and Negative Meaning.** Fill in the diagram with the adjectives in the box. Decide which adjectives describe personalities positively, negatively, or both. Add other adjectives you know.

annoying	funny	lovable	outgoing	silly
easygoing	hardworking	modest	professional	smart
friendly	helpful	nervous	reliable	talkative
fun	impolite	offensive	serious	unfair

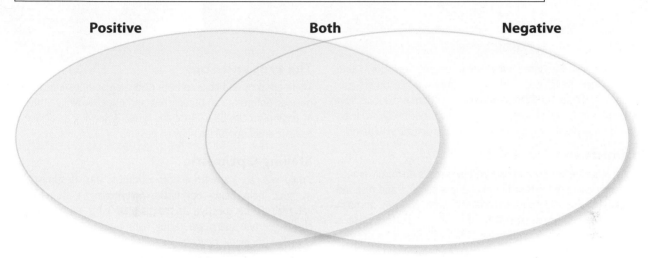

Positive   Both   Negative

E **Associate Words and Ideas.** With a partner, write adjectives from the chart you think match each of the personality types. More than one answer is possible. Explain your choices.

1. a sweetheart ....
2. a team player ....
3. a brain ....
4. a pain in the neck ....
5. a tyrant ....
6. a wise guy ....
7. a people person ....
8. a workaholic ....

NOW YOU CAN *Describe people's personalities*

A **Use the Vocabulary.** Describe the personalities of people you know. Give specific examples to explain.

> *"My sister is such **a tyrant**! She makes her kids do all the housework!"*

> *"My friend Hugo is **a real people person**. He's so outgoing and friendly."*

IDEAS

a boss	a friend
a co-worker	a neighbor
a spouse	a teacher
a classmate	a relative

B **Use the Conversation Strategies.** Role-play a conversation about a person you haven't met yet. Use the Conversation Snapshot as a guide. Start like this: "Have you had a chance to meet . . . ?"

3 GOAL
Compare perspectives on life

A **Reading Warm-up.** Look at the glass of water. Do you see the glass as half full or half empty? What does that say about your perspective on life?

B 🎧 **Reading.** Read the article about optimism. How do optimists and pessimists respond to problems differently?

Maintaining a Positive Perspective

by Kali Munro, M.Ed., Psychotherapist

Have you ever wondered why some people feel down and defeated when faced with difficult situations, while others feel challenged and hopeful? These different reactions are due to how people interpret events—whether they think positively, from an optimistic viewpoint, or negatively, from a pessimistic viewpoint.

Optimists and Pessimists

The difference between optimists and pessimists isn't a difference in life experiences but rather in how people perceive and respond to problems. For example, an optimist who is going through a hard time feels confident that life will get better, while a pessimist is more cynical and believes life will always be difficult and painful. Pessimists tend to expect the worst and see only problems. Optimists, confronted with the same situations, expect the best. While a pessimist may give up, an optimist will look on the bright side and, instead of seeing a problem, will see a solution.

The Pros and Cons

There are pros and cons to both optimism and pessimism. A healthy dose of optimism can be uplifting and hopeful, while a healthy dose of pessimism can be realistic and wise. Achieving a balance of being realistic and hopeful isn't always easy.

Staying Optimistic

While we can learn from both optimists and pessimists, most of us need help being optimistic. Maintaining a hopeful, positive, yet realistic perspective in the face of hard times can be a real challenge—one many are facing right now in the world—but it is essential to living peacefully and happily. Just as it is important to recognize what is unjust and unfair in our lives and the world, it is important to see the beauty, love, generosity, and goodness as well.

> On your ActiveBook disc: *Reading Glossary* and *Extra Reading Comprehension Questions*

Information source: www.KaliMunro.com

C **Relate to Personal Experience.** Discuss the questions.

1. Do you agree with the author that "most of us need help being optimistic"? How do you think people can avoid negative thinking? Describe experiences from your own life.

2. In your opinion, are there times when optimism can be bad, or when pessimism can be good? Explain.

D **Identify Supporting Details.** With a partner, rate these people's optimisim on a scale of 1 to 5 (1 being very optimistic and 5 being very pessimistic). Explain your answers, citing information from the article.

I wouldn't say that I'm cynical, but it's important to be realistic. Let's face it—life is hard.

1 2 3 4 5

I think I can keep things in perspective. I try not to think negatively, but I'm realistic about the things I can't change.

1 2 3 4 5

I try to look on the bright side. I think it's better to try to see a solution instead of seeing a problem.

1 2 3 4 5

I find it difficult when things get tough. I sometimes feel completely hopeless. I just don't expect things to get better.

1 2 3 4 5

I've had some bad experiences, but I think they've made me more realistic. It's not always possible to hope for the best, but good things *do* happen.

1 2 3 4 5

A **Frame Your Ideas.** Complete the survey.

Do you have a negative or positive perspective?

1. You wake up in the middle of the night with a stomachache. Your first thought is . . .

- **1pt** "I'm sure it's nothing."
- **2pts** "I'll take some medicine."
- **3pts** "I think I should go to the doctor."

2. You apply for your "perfect" job, but you don't get it. You think . . .

- **1pt** "Never mind. I'll find something else."
- **2pts** "That's really unfair."
- **3pts** "It figures. I never get the job I want."

3. When you are introduced to someone new, you . . .

- **1pt** make friends easily with that person.
- **2pts** "warm up" to that person gradually.
- **3pts** make that person prove to you that he or she is likable.

4. News about crime or disasters makes you . . .

- **1pt** want to do something to help.
- **2pts** realize that sometimes bad things happen.
- **3pts** feel unsafe and depressed.

5. When a friend feels down, you . . .

- **1pt** understand and try to offer support.
- **2pts** tell him or her about your problems too.
- **3pts** tell him or her how much worse it could be.

6. Your boss asks you out to lunch. You think . . .

- **1pt** "I must be getting a raise."
- **2pts** "That's really nice."
- **3pts** "Oh, no! I'm getting fired!"

7. If someone unexpectedly knocks on your door, you think . . .

- **1pt** "I wonder which friend is dropping by."
- **2pts** "I wonder who it could be."
- **3pts** "I'm not answering. It must be a salesperson."

> **Add up your points.**
> 7–10   You're an optimist. You always see the glass half full.
> 11–14   You're a bit of an optimist and a pessimist. You're very realistic.
> 15–21   You're a pessimist. You tend to see the glass half empty.

B **Draw Conclusions.** With a partner, compare and explain your responses to the survey items. Does your score describe you and your perspective on life? Why or why not?

C **Discussion.**

1. In your opinion, in order to succeed, how important is your perspective on life? Do you think it's better to be optimistic, pessimistic, or somewhere in the middle? Explain.

2. Read the quotation by Winston Churchill. Do you agree with him? Why or why not?

"The pessimist sees difficulty in every opportunity. The optimist sees the opportunity in every difficulty."

Winston Churchill,
British Prime Minister
(1874–1965)

GOAL
4
Share a life-changing experience

A 🎧 1:09 **Listening. Listen for Main Ideas.** Listen to each person talking about a life-changing experience. Then choose the best answer to complete each statement.

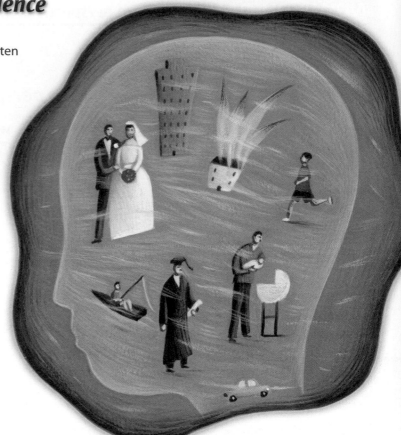

1. The most significant experience of the first speaker's life was when he _____.
   a. became a father
   b. began working
   c. traveled to another country
   d. got married

2. The second speaker's life changed when she _____.
   a. got a full-time job
   b. had a baby
   c. got more free time
   d. got married

3. The third speaker's perspective on life changed when he _____.
   a. lost his home in a fire
   b. lost his job
   c. got divorced
   d. had a serious illness

B 🎧 1:10 **Listening. Understand from Context.** Read the statements. Then listen again to infer what each speaker means.

1. When the first speaker says, "I was really able to see other people's points of view," he means that _____.
   a. he could understand how other people feel about things
   b. he met people of different nationalities

2. When the first speaker says, "It was a real eye-opener for me," he means that _____.
   a. the experience was a bit scary
   b. the experience taught him a lot

3. When the second speaker says, "It hit me that I was responsible for her," she means that _____.
   a. she realized she had to take care of her baby
   b. she regretted she had to take care of her baby

4. When the second speaker says, "[It] is definitely a life-altering experience," she means that _____.
   a. the experience is not rewarding
   b. the experience changes a person

5. When the third speaker says, "That put things in perspective," he means that _____.
   a. he realized some things are not so important
   b. he had to work day in and day out

6. When the third speaker says, "You start to see the big picture," he means that _____.
   a. he understood what was really important in life
   b. he realized how much he had lost

C **Summarize.** First, in your own words, summarize each person's life-changing experience. Then discuss which person's experience you identify with the most. Explain why.

A **Pair Work.** Explore ideas about experiences that can change a person's perspective on life. Complete the list with your partner.

> **Things that can change one's perspective**
> -the birth of a child
> -a disaster
> -travel
> ....
> ....
> ....
> ....
> ....

B **Notepadding.** Think about a life-changing experience *you* have had. Take notes about it on your notepad.

What was the experience? When did it happen? Where?

How did the experience change your perspective? How did you feel at the time?

C **Group Work.** Share your life-changing experience with your classmates. Explain how this experience changed your perspective on life.

> "Last year my mother had a serious illness. It really put things in perspective for me. All the disagreements we'd had in the past seemed so unimportant."

> "A few years ago, I went on vacation to Europe. It hit me how useful it was knowing English. It came in handy in a lot of situations."

D **Presentation.** Write a paragraph about a life-changing experience you have had. Use it to present your story to your class or group.

Writing: Describe personality types

Paragraph Structure: Review

A paragraph consists of sentences about one topic. The most important sentence in a paragraph is the **topic sentence**. It is usually the first sentence, and it introduces the topic of a paragraph. For example:

Workaholics lead unbalanced lives.

In academic writing, all the **supporting sentences** that follow a topic sentence—details, examples, and other facts—must be related to the topic presented in the topic sentence.

The last sentence of the paragraph is often a **concluding sentence**. A concluding sentence restates the topic sentence or summarizes the paragraph. A concluding sentence often includes phrases such as In conclusion or In summary.

WRITING MODEL

Workaholics lead unbalanced lives. They spend all their energy on work. They rarely take time to relax and let their minds rest. I know because my father was a workaholic, and he worked every day of the week. We hardly ever saw him. Even when he was not at work, we knew he was thinking about work. He seemed never to think of anything else. In summary, not knowing how to escape from work makes it difficult for a workaholic to find balance in his or her life.

A **Prewriting. Brainstorming Ideas.** Write a topic sentence for each personality type.

team players	tyrants	wise guys

1. ....

2. ....

3. ....

Now choose one of your topic sentences. On a separate sheet of paper, generate ideas you could use to support the topic.

Workaholics lead unbalanced lives.
—always think about work
—can't relax

B **Writing.** On a separate sheet of paper, write a paragraph about the personality type you chose in Prewriting. Make sure all the supporting sentences relate to the topic. End with a concluding sentence.

C **Self-Check.**

☐ Does your paragraph have a topic sentence?
☐ Do the supporting sentences in your paragraph all relate to the topic?
☐ Do you have a concluding sentence?

ActiveBook: More Practice

grammar · vocabulary · listening
reading · speaking · pronunciation

A 🎧 **Listening.** Listen to the people talking about their reactions to events in the news. Decide if each speaker is an optimist, a pessimist, or a realist.

1. John ....   **2.** Susan ....   **3.** Matt ....

B Now read the statements. Write the name of the person from the listening who is most likely to have said each statement. Listen again if necessary.

1. "You've got to be practical. There will be some problems in life that you can solve and some that you can't. What's important is realizing when something is beyond your control. Then it's better just to move on." ....

2. "Life is full of hard times. You just have to accept the fact that bad things happen and know that there's very little you can do about it." ....

3. "It's important to see a problem as both a challenge to be faced and as an opportunity for success. Difficult experiences can make a person stronger." ....

C Complete each conversation with a personality type.

1. **A:** Looks like I have to work overtime again tonight. My supervisor just gave me three projects to complete by the end of the day.
    B: You're kidding. He sounds like a real ....!

2. **A:** You know, without Sarah's help, I would never have completed that presentation in time.
    B: Tell me about it. She really helped me out with my sales campaign last month. She's such a ....

3. **A:** Tom is really a .... I ran into him in the park last weekend, and he was sitting on a bench and working on that report.
    B: Yeah, that's Tom all right. He never stops!

4. **A:** I don't think Jill had a very good time at the party—she didn't say a word the whole evening.
    B: Well, Jill doesn't feel comfortable in social situations. She's just not a ....

5. **A:** Have you heard the news? My daughter Audrey got a perfect score on her entrance exam to law school.
    B: Congratulations! I always knew she would do well in school. She's such a ....

6. **A:** I'm so tired of Ken. The other day I made a mistake at the computer lab at school, and he said something that really made me feel dumb.
    B: Don't let it get to you. Everybody knows he's a .... Just try to ignore him.

D On a separate sheet of paper, write advice for each person. Use the verbs <u>stop</u>, <u>remember</u>, and <u>forget</u> with gerunds or infinitives.

She should stop working so much.

1. Samantha has a demanding job and works long hours. When she finally gets home, she's exhausted. She spends all weekend trying to catch up on housework and shopping.

2. Michael spends most of the day at the computer. Some days he doesn't even get outside except to walk to the bus stop. On the weekends, he just watches a lot of TV.

3. Philip is a single father with three kids, and he travels a lot for his company. He feels his kids are growing up so fast that he hardly ever sees them.

4. Marisa has been using her credit cards a lot lately, and she can't keep up with the monthly payments. And now she's having a hard time keeping up with *all* her bills.

Musical Moods

GOALS After Unit 2, you will be able to:

1 Describe the music you listen to
2 Explain the role of music in your life
3 Describe a creative person
4 Discuss the benefits of music

A **Topic Preview.** Look at the reviews from the music website.
Are you familiar with any of these artists?

TUNE IN
0 1 2 3 4 5 6 7 8 9 10

Artist ⬍ Go Search

Today's Picks

Home
New Releases
Explore by...
  genre
  instrument
  artist
Editor's Choice
Top Searches
Site Guide
Newsletter
About Us
Subscribe

LATIN

Carlos Ponce, *Ponce*
Puerto Rican singer /
songwriter (and TV star)
Carlos Ponce delivers a fun
mix of romantic ballads
and Caribbean-flavored
dance grooves. Even if you
don't understand Spanish,
you can't help but feel the
emotion in Ponce's voice,
which ranges from a rough
growl to a passionate cry.

JAZZ

marcos ariel

my only passion

Marcos Ariel, *My Only Passion*
Another brilliant set from
the richly talented Brazilian
keyboardist / composer
Marcos Ariel. Check out the
unpredictable interplay
between the group members
in "Bahia Suite," where Meia
Noite's exciting percussion
sets the tempo, while Ariel's
piano races in and around
Frank Gambale's surprising
guitar lines.

POP

ANDREA BOCELLI SOGNO

Andrea Bocelli, *Sogno*
Sogno finds the classically
trained Bocelli moving
away from the world of
opera with a collection
of modern pop ballads.
Fans of Bocelli's
remarkable voice won't
be disappointed. Whether
he's singing an Italian
pop song or a lovely duet
with pop diva Celine
Dion, the depth and
feeling of his music will
touch your soul.

NEW AGE

KITARO

BEST OF SILK ROAD

Kitaro, *Best of Silk Road*
Described as "sound pictures"
and "mind music" in his native
Japan, Kitaro's electronic music
incorporates the sounds of
waves, wind, and rain, inspiring
listeners to feel and appreciate
the natural world. A true
masterpiece.

URBAN DANCE

Beyoncé
dangerously in love

Beyoncé, *Dangerously in Love*
Beyoncé kicks off her solo
career and keeps the dance
floors crowded with her hit
singles on this energetic
recording. Hear the red-hot
"Crazy in Love" (a duet with
rap artist Jay-Z) and the playful
"Baby Boy" (with dance-hall star
Sean Paul) just once and you'll
be humming them in your
head all day.

WORLD

MUZSIKÁS
THE PRISONER'S SONG

Muzsikás, *The Prisoner's Song*
Singing in Hungarian and
playing traditional
instruments, Muzsikás
arranges ten Eastern
European folk songs to tell a
haunting story of love, desire,
and freedom. Add lead singer
Márta Sebestyén's amazing
voice, and you've got a sound
unlike any you've ever heard.

Information source: www.allmusic.com

B **Express Your Ideas.**

1. Which reviews did you find the most appealing? Why? Which musical genres in the reviews
   interest you the most?
2. Can you think of other artists for each genre?

C 1:12 🎧 **Sound Bites.** Read and listen
to a conversation between two friends
comparing musical tastes.

TANIA: Wow! You've got quite a CD collection!
KEN: I guess so. Let's put something on.
TANIA: Got any jazz?
KEN: How about some Gato Barbieri? I've got
Fenix.
TANIA: Actually, his saxophone playing kind of
gets on my nerves on that one.
KEN: Really? I'm totally into him. *Fenix* is one of
my all-time favorites.
TANIA: Yeah, but it's pretty hard to dance to.
KEN: Well, have you heard some of his later stuff?
TANIA: No, what's it like?
KEN: It's got more of a Latin feel. It'll definitely
get the party started.
TANIA: Oh yeah? Let's give it a listen.

D **Think and Explain.** Read the
conversation again. With a partner, explain
the meaning of each of the following
statements or questions.

1. "You've got quite a CD collection."
2. "Let's put something on."
3. "His saxophone playing kind of gets on my nerves on that one."
4. "I'm totally into him."
5. "Have you heard some of his later stuff?"
6. "It'll definitely get the party started."
7. "Let's give it a listen."

STARTING **POINT**

A **Frame Your Ideas.** What recordings are your all-time favorites? Complete the chart.

Title of recording	Artist or group	Genre of music

B **Pair Work.** Talk with a partner
about the music in your chart.
Compare your musical tastes.

*"I'm totally into Coldplay.
That CD is fantastic!"*

*"Well, rock usually gets on my nerves,
but maybe I'll give it a listen sometime."*

1

GOAL
Describe the music you listen to

Youssou N'Dour

A 🎧 **Conversation Snapshot.** Read and listen. Notice the conversation strategies.

1:13

A: **So** what have you been listening to lately?

B: Mostly world music. Ever heard of Youssou N'Dour?

A: I think so. He's from Senegal, **right**?

B: That's right.

A: **You know,** I've actually never heard his music. What's he like?

B: **Well,** he's got a terrific voice and a unique sound. I'd be happy to lend you a CD if you'd like.

A: All right, thanks. I'll let you know what I think.

1:14
🎧 **Rhythm and intonation practice**

B 🎧 **Vocabulary. Elements of Music.** Listen and practice.

1:15

beat the rhythm of a piece of music
That song has a great beat you can dance to.

lyrics the words of a song
Her catchy lyrics make you want to sing along.

melody the order of notes in a musical piece
His song has an unforgettable melody.

sound the particular style or quality of an artist's or group's music
The band has created a new and exciting sound.

voice the quality of sound produced when one sings
She has a beautiful soprano voice.

C 🎧 **Listening. Listen to Activate Vocabulary.** Listen to the pieces of music. With a partner, use the words from the Vocabulary to discuss what you like or don't like about the music.

1:16

PRONUNCIATION BOOSTER ▸ p. P2
• Intonation patterns

D **Grammar. The present perfect and the present perfect continuous: finished and unfinished actions**

Finished actions
Use the present perfect, not the present perfect continuous, when an action is completed at an unspecified time in the past. (Remember that actions completed at a specified time in the past require the simple past tense.)
I**'ve** already **heard** that CD. I heard it yesterday.
How many times **have** you **seen** Youssou N'Dour in concert?
I**'ve seen** him twice. As a matter of fact, I just saw him last week.

Very recently finished actions: an exception
The present perfect continuous is preferred to describe very recently completed actions when results can still be seen.
They**'ve been practicing**. I see them putting their instruments away.

Unfinished or continuing actions
Use the present perfect OR the present perfect continuous to describe actions that began in the past, continue into the present, and may continue into the future.
Have you **listened** to any jazz lately? OR **Have** you **been listening** to any jazz lately?
I**'ve listened** to Beethoven since I was a child. OR I**'ve been listening** to Beethoven since I was a child.

Words and phrases used with the present perfect for finished actions
already ever never yet
once, twice, three times
How many . . . ?

Words and expressions often used with unfinished actions
for   lately   these days
since   recently   for a while
all day this year   How long . . . ?

GRAMMAR BOOSTER ▸ p. G3
• Finished and unfinished actions: summary
• The past perfect continuous

E Grammar Practice. Write <u>F</u> if the action is finished. Write <u>U</u> if the action is unfinished or continuing.

.... **1.** He's played with their band for almost ten years.

.... **2.** Caetano Veloso has made dozens of recordings.

.... **3.** They've never heard of Alexandre Pires.

.... **4.** We've been listening to that CD all day. Let's play something different.

.... **5.** Ladysmith Black Mambazo hasn't been playing many concerts lately.

.... **6.** Have you ever gone to a classical concert?

.... **7.** How many times have you heard Carmina Burana?

.... **8.** They've played Brahms's First Symphony twice this year.

F Grammar Practice. Complete the biography of Vanessa-Mae with the simple past tense, the present perfect, or the present perfect continuous. Use the present perfect continuous if the action is unfinished or continuing.

Vanessa-Mae

Vanessa-Mae .... music since she was a little girl.
                            (1. perform)
Born in Singapore on October 27, 1978, she .... her
                                              (2. have)
first piano lesson at the age of three. A year later, she ....
                                                           (3. start)
taking violin lessons, and when she was just ten years old, she

.... her concert debut with the London Philharmonic.
    (4. make)
    Since then, Vanessa-Mae .... numerous classical
                                (5. make)
recordings, but it was in 1994 that she .... the field of
                                           (6. enter)
pop music with *The Violin Player*. The album immediately .... extremely
                                                              (7. become)
popular with pop and classical music fans.

    In more recent years, she .... with other pop artists such as Annie Lennox,
                                 (8. play)
Janet Jackson, and Prince. Vanessa-Mae .... her audiences for over a decade,
                                            (9. entertain)
and she continues to astonish them with her innovative sound.

NOW YOU CAN *Describe the music you listen to*

A Notepadding. Write some of the musical artists or bands you've been listening to lately.

Artist or band	What you like
Étoile de Dakar	great dance beat

Artist or band	What you like

B Use the Conversation Strategies. Talk about music you listen to. Use the Vocabulary from page 16 and the Conversation Snapshot as a guide. Start like this: "So what have you been listening to lately?"

Explain the role of music in your life

A 🎧 1:17 **Grammar Snapshot.** Read the commentaries and notice the noun clauses.

Frankly, I can't imagine **what my life would be like without music**. It's **what gets me through the day**. Listening to music is **how I get going in the morning**. Later, at work, it's **how I stay productive**. And in the evening, it's **what helps me unwind**.

Patricia Nichols, 34
Vancouver, Canada

It's my opinion **that music is a kind of international language**—a way for people to communicate with **whomever they meet**. The fact **that enjoyment of music is universal** makes it an ideal way to bring cultures together. Music can open doors for you everywhere you go in the world.

Santigi Matomi, 27
Freetown, Sierra Leone

I'm a performer, and music is a part of who I am. It's a way for me to express **what's in my heart**. The truth is, **whether or not I perform** is not really a choice—I have to do it. **Whatever happens during the day**—good or bad—comes out in my music.

Alison Wu, 19
Shanghai, China

B **Make Personal Comparisons.** Do any of the comments above ring true for you? Explain and discuss.

C **Grammar. Noun clauses**

A noun clause can be a subject, a direct object, an indirect object, a subject complement, or the object of a preposition.

> **Whatever happens during the day** comes out in my music. [subject]
> I don't know **why I'm so crazy about his music**. [direct object]
> I'll give **whoever calls first** the tickets. [indirect object]
> Music is **what helps me unwind**. [subject complement]
> Music is a way for people to communicate with **whomever* they meet**. [object of a preposition]

Indirect speech is expressed using a noun clause.

> They asked **whether / if we could recommend some good recordings**.
> The violinist explained **that the concerto was quite difficult to play**.

A noun clause can also be introduced by whoever, whomever, or whatever, meaning any person or any thing.

> **Whoever can combine hip-hop with pop** is sure to be a hit.
> The audience always loves **whatever they play**.

Noun clauses often follow phrases with impersonal It subjects.

> It's my opinion **that music is a kind of international language**.

In writing, subject noun clauses are often preceded by phrases such as the fact, the idea, etc.

> The fact **that enjoyment of music is universal** is quite interesting.

*very formal

REMEMBER

A noun clause can begin with <u>that</u>, <u>if</u>, <u>whether (or not)</u>, or a question word.

> I believe **that** life would be empty without music.
> We asked them **if** they could play the song for us again.
> OR We asked them **whether (or not)** they could play the song for us again.
> I'm not sure **why** the band decided to break up.
> Do you know **which / what** instrument she plays?
> They asked her **how** she trained her voice to be so beautiful.

When a noun clause is a direct object, the word <u>that</u> may be omitted.

> I believe life would be empty without music.

BE CAREFUL! Use normal, not inverted, word order in noun clauses beginning with question words.

> NOT They asked her how ~~did she~~ ~~train~~ her voice to be so beautiful.

GRAMMAR BOOSTER
► p. G4
• Noun clauses as adjective and noun complements

D **Grammar Practice.** Introduce each noun clause with <u>that</u>, <u>if</u>, <u>whether</u> (<u>or not</u>), or a question word.

Question words	
who	what
why	which
when	how
where	

1. It's his opinion .... classical music is boring.
2. Buying old records is .... I spend my Saturday afternoons.
3. I'm having difficulty recalling .... band played at the dance.
4. .... I like most is to take a hot bath while I listen to music.
5. Did they tell you .... the concert would start? I don't want to be late.
6. I can't really tell you .... I like some pieces of music. Maybe it's because they remind me of songs my mother sang to me when I was a child.
7. Robert asked me .... I had bought tickets yet.
8. She can't imagine .... she would do without music.

E **Grammar Practice.** Complete each statement with a noun clause that represents each question.

1. I don't know ....
(Where did Mozart live?)

2. I have no idea ....
(When did Georges Bizet compose Carmen?)

3. She told me ....
(Where do the Black Sheep usually perform?)

4. I don't know ....
(Which genre of music is his favorite?)

5. I'm not sure ....
(What kind of lyrics does she write?)

NOW YOU CAN   *Explain the role of music in your life*

A **Analyze the Grammar.** Read the following quotations and underline the noun clauses. Classify each noun clause by its grammatical function within the sentence (subject, direct object, etc.). Then discuss the meaning of each quotation. Restate each in your own words.

> *"The audience knows when they're just listening to notes and when they're truly listening to music."*
> **Sarah Chang**, U.S. violinist
> 1980 –

> *"Music is a gift and a burden I've had since I can remember who I was."*
> **Nina Simone**, U.S. singer and pianist
> 1933 – 2003

> *"What I have in my heart must come out. This is why I compose music."*
> **Ludwig van Beethoven**, German composer
> 1770 – 1827

B **Use the Grammar.** Discuss the role of music in your life. Do you listen to music at specific times during your day? What sorts of music do you listen to? Use noun clauses to explain your ideas.

Listening to music is . . .
I can't imagine . . .
It's my opinion . . .

A 🎧 1:18 **Vocabulary. Describing Creative Personalities.** Listen and practice.

Positive qualities

gifted having a natural ability to do one or more things extremely well
energetic very active, physically and mentally
imaginative able to think of new and interesting ideas
passionate showing a strong liking for something and being very dedicated to it

Negative qualities

eccentric behaving in an unusual way or appearing different from most people
difficult never satisfied and hard to please
moody quickly and easily becoming annoyed or unhappy
egotistical believing oneself to be better or more important than other people

B **Reading Warm-up.** It is often said that gifted people have eccentric or difficult personalities. Do you agree?

C 🎧 1:19 **Reading.** Read the short biography. What effect did Beethoven's personality have on his life?

On your ActiveBook disc: *Reading Glossary* and *Extra Reading Comprehension Questions*

Ludwig van Beethoven:
A Passion for Music

Born in 1770 in Bonn, Germany, Ludwig van Beethoven started playing the piano before he was four years old. By the time he was twelve, this child prodigy had already composed his first piece of music. When Beethoven was just sixteen, he went to study in Vienna, Austria, then the center of European cultural life and home to the most brilliant and passionate musicians and composers of the period. Beethoven proved to be a gifted pianist and an imaginative composer.

Beethoven is remembered for his great genius but also for his strong and difficult personality. In one infamous incident, Beethoven became so upset with a waiter that he emptied a plate of food over the man's head. Despite this type of behavior, many in musical and aristocratic circles admired Beethoven, and music lovers were always Beethoven's greatest supporters. This fact did not prevent him from losing his temper with one or another of them. However, because of his talent, Beethoven's friends always excused his insults and moody temperament.

Beethoven was also notorious for his eccentric behavior. He often walked through the streets of Vienna muttering to himself and stamping his feet. He completely neglected his personal appearance; his clothes would get so dirty that his friends would come and take them away during the night. When they replaced the old clothes with new ones, Beethoven never noticed the difference.

Although Beethoven was respected and admired by his audience, he was not concerned with pleasing them. Beethoven could play the piano so beautifully that some listeners cried; however, when he saw his fans crying, Beethoven only laughed and said they were fools. He was so egotistical that if people talked while he was performing, he would stop and walk away.

Beethoven wrote two famous works, *Moonlight Sonata* and *Für Elise*, for two different women he loved. He was almost always in love, often with a woman who was already married or engaged. Although Beethoven asked several women to marry him, they all rejected him. But the most tragic aspect of Beethoven's life was his gradual loss of hearing, beginning in his late twenties until he was completely deaf. However, even as his hearing grew worse, Beethoven continued to be energetic and productive; his creative activity remained intense, and audiences loved his music. In 1826, Beethoven held his last public performance of his famous Ninth Symphony. By this time, the maestro was completely deaf. When he was turned around so he could see the roaring applause that he could not hear, Beethoven began to cry.

Beethoven died in Vienna in 1827 at age fifty-seven. One out of ten people who lived in Vienna came to his funeral.

Information source: www.classicalarchive.com

D **Activate Language from a Text.** Read each fact about Beethoven. Then, with a partner, discuss which adjective from the Vocabulary best completes each statement.

1. Beethoven was already publishing music and earning a salary at the age of twelve. He was very ....

2. Beethoven once told a prince, "There will be thousands of princes. There is only one Beethoven." He could be quite ....

3. Beethoven would work long hours composing and never seemed to tire. He was always .... when he performed for his audiences.

4. Beethoven had many close friends who tried to help him with his problems. He continually pushed them away and refused their assistance. He was considered to be a .... person.

5. Beethoven became frustrated when he began to lose his hearing. While socializing with his friends, he would often have sudden bursts of anger. He could be rather ....

6. Beethoven said that his music expressed what was inside of him and that he had no choice but to compose. He was a .... composer.

7. Beethoven's attention to feeling in his music began a new "style," different in some ways from Baroque music, which was popular at the time. His compositions were ....

8. Beethoven's friends thought he could be .... at times. For example, when he made coffee, he used to count out exactly sixty beans for each cup.

NOW YOU CAN *Describe a creative person*

A **Frame Your Ideas.** Rate your own personality on a scale of 0 to 3. Compare your answers with a partner's. Use the Vocabulary.

> "I'm an extremely **passionate** person. I think it's really important to love what you do. What about you?"

0 = not at all	1 = a little	2 = somewhat	3 = extremely	
gifted ◯	eccentric ◯	passionate ◯	imaginative ◯	
difficult ◯	energetic ◯	moody ◯	egotistical ◯	creative ◯

B **Discussion.** Read the quotations from three famous musicians. Which one do you find the most interesting? After reading the quotations, how would you describe each musician's personality?

"Music is nothing separate from me. It is me. . . . You'd have to remove the music surgically."

Ray Charles, American soul singer, songwriter, and pianist, 1930–2004

"Music will save the world."

Pablo Casals, Spanish cellist and conductor, 1876–1973

"I've outdone anyone you can name—Mozart, Beethoven, Bach, Strauss. Irving Berlin, he wrote 1,001 tunes. I wrote 5,500."

James Brown, American R & B singer and songwriter, 1933–2006

C **Project.** Write a brief biography of a creative person you know. Describe his or her personality, creativity, and achievements. Put all the biographies together for a web article about creative people.

4

Discuss the benefits of music

A 🎧 **Listening. Listen for Main Ideas.** Read the questions. Then listen to Part 1 of a talk about an unusual use of music. Discuss the questions with a partner.

1:20

1. What does Dr. Schmidt do?
2. What sorts of people does she work with? Explain how she works with these people.

B 🎧 **Listening. Listen for Supporting Details.** Read the questions. Then listen to Part 2 of the talk and answer the questions.

1:21

1. What are the four benefits Dr. Schmidt talks about?
   a. ....
   b. ....
   c. ....
   d. ....

2. What is one example of each?
   a. ....
   b. ....
   c. ....
   d. ....

C **Apply Ideas.** Discuss the questions.

1. Can you think of any other benefits of music therapy?
2. Can you think of anyone who might benefit from music therapy? If so, how?

D Word Skills. Using Participial Adjectives.

The present and past participle forms of many verbs function as adjectives.

The past participle has a passive meaning. Most sentences using past participles can be restated with a **by** phrase.

> The patient is **depressed**. = The patient is depressed [by his life].
> I'm **bored**. = I'm bored [by this movie].

The present participle does not have a passive meaning. Most sentences using present participles can be restated with an active verb.

> That book is **depressing**. = That book depresses [everyone].
> It's so **boring**. = It bores [me].

1:22
🎧 | Present participles | Past participles
--- | ---
amazing | amazed
annoying | annoyed
boring | bored
depressing | depressed
disappointing | disappointed
entertaining | entertained
exciting | excited
interesting | interested
pleasing | pleased
relaxing | relaxed
soothing | soothed
stimulating | stimulated
touching | touched

E Word Skills Practice. Circle an adjective to complete the sentence about music therapy.

1. Music can make patients feel (relaxed / relaxing).
2. Listening to music makes patients feel less (depressed / depressing).
3. Patients find some types of music to be very (soothed / soothing).
4. For patients in physical pain, the benefits of music can be (surprised / surprising).
5. Studies show that a student's ability to learn is (stimulated / stimulating) by music.
6. For patients with emotional problems, music can be very (comforted / comforting).
7. Many doctors report they are (pleased / pleasing) by the effect music has on their patients.
8. Many patients say that music therapy is (entertained / entertaining).

NOW YOU CAN   *Discuss the benefits of music*

A Notepadding. What are some benefits music brings to people's lives? With a partner, make a list and discuss. Use participial adjectives.

Benefits	Examples
Music can be soothing.	Playing music at work can relax people so they're more productive.

Benefits	Examples

B Group Work. Share your ideas with your class or group. Comment on your classmates' ideas.

23

Writing: Describe yourself

Parallel Structure

In a pair or a series, be sure to use parallel structure. All the words, phrases, or clauses should be in the same form.

Incorrect	Correct
He's a composer, singer, and a violinist. (article, no article, article)	He's **a** composer, **a** singer, and **a** violinist. (article, article, article) OR He's **a** composer, singer, and violinist. (one article for all three)
I like dancing, painting, and to sing. (gerund, gerund, infinitive)	I like **dancing, painting**, and **singing**. (gerund, gerund, gerund) OR I like **to dance, to paint**, and **to sing**. (infinitive, infinitive, infinitive) OR I like **to dance, paint**, and **sing**. (one to for all three)
The picture was framed, examined, and they sold it. (passive, passive, active)	The picture was **framed, examined**, and **sold**. (passive, passive, passive)
I like people who have the same interests as I do, make me laugh, or who like outdoor sports. (clause, verb phrase, clause)	I like people **who have the same interests as I do, who make me laugh**, or **who like outdoor sports**. (clause, clause, clause) OR I like people who **have the same interests as I do, make me laugh**, or **like outdoor sports**. (verb phrase, verb phrase, verb phrase)

A Prewriting. Clustering Ideas.
Look at the idea cluster below. On a separate sheet of paper, create your own idea cluster. Draw a circle and write ME inside it. Then write any ideas that come to mind in circles around the main circle. Expand each new idea. Include hobbies, accomplishments, places you have traveled, interests, goals, etc.

Example

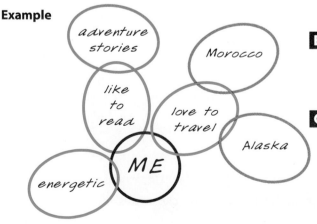

ERROR CORRECTION | Correct the errors.

I have always been a relaxed, passionate, and been a moody person. I love traveling, to meet new people, and learning about new places. I have been to many interesting places; for example, I have been on top of Mount Kilimanjaro, I have gone ice fishing with Eskimos in Alaska, and I rode on a camel in Morocco. These were some of

B Writing.
On a separate sheet of paper, write a paragraph describing yourself, using the information from your cluster. Make sure to use parallel structure.

C Self-Check.
☐ Did you use parallel structure with pairs or series of nouns, adjectives, and adverbs?

☐ Did you use parallel structure with the clauses, phrases, and tenses?

☐ Does the topic sentence introduce the topic of the paragraph?

Review

A 🎧 **Listening.** Listen to the conversations about musical preferences.
Determine if each person likes the artist or group. Check the appropriate box or boxes.
Then listen again and write what the person likes (voice, melody, lyrics, beat, or sound).

	the man	the woman	what he or she likes
1. Andrea Bocelli	☐	☐	....
2. Gato Barbieri	☐	☐	....
3. Ladysmith Black Mambazo	☐	☐	....
4. Beyoncé	☐	☐	....
5. Antonio Carlos Jobim	☐	☐	....

B Complete the statements with an appropriate adjective from the box.

eccentric	egotistical	energetic	gifted	moody	passionate

1. Sarah is a very .... musician. She started playing the piano when she was three.

2. My neighbor has thirty cats. You could say he's a bit ....

3. Franco is an extremely .... person. He only thinks of himself.

4. Dalia is so .... lately. She gets angry at the smallest thing.

C Circle the correct form of the verb to complete the paragraph.

Sandile Khemese (**1.** has played / played) the violin since he was a child in Johannesburg,
South Africa. In 1989, Sandile (**2.** formed / has formed) the Soweto String Quartet with
his brothers, Reuben and Thami, and their friend, Makhosini Mnguni. The group
(**3.** played / has played) at President Nelson Mandela's inauguration in 1994. The Soweto
String Quartet (**4.** won / has won) many music awards in South Africa, including Best New
Artist. They (**5.** have recorded / have been recording) a number of successful CDs. In recent
years, the Quartet (**6.** has been giving / gave) concerts all around the world.

D Underline the noun clause in each sentence. Write whether it is a subject, a direct object,
a subject complement, or an object of a preposition.

1. I believe that without music life wouldn't be as much fun. ....

2. Whatever's playing on the radio is fine with me. ....

3. That's why Jorge likes only pop music. ....

4. Do you know where some good music is playing? ....

5. They'll listen to whatever music is playing. ....

Money Matters

GOALS After Unit 3, you will be able to:

1 Talk about your financial goals
2 Express buyer's remorse
3 Describe your spending habits
4 Discuss reasons for charitable giving

A **Topic Preview.** Read these financial tips.
Do you think you have a high financial IQ?

How to Raise Your Financial IQ

1. Save money.

Start saving while you are young. When you have money in your pocket, the impulse to spend it can be very strong. When you get your paycheck, don't run to the mall. If you put away a small amount of money into a savings account each week and earn interest, your money will grow.

2. Live within your means.

The secret to financial success is spending less than you earn. If you make a lot of money, but spend it all, you are not really rich or financially secure. If you lose your job, or get seriously ill, you will have nothing to fall back on. People who make less money than you but don't spend it all are actually much wealthier because they are able to handle any emergency that arises. Fortunately, today's technology makes managing your money easier than ever. Financial-planning software can help you keep a budget by adding up your income and expenses and keeping track of your spending.

3. Don't go into debt.

It is a lot easier—and sometimes safer—to pay with a credit card than to carry around a lot of cash in your pocket or purse. However, it is easy to get into trouble with credit cards if you use them as a substitute for money you don't have. If you charge so much that you can't keep up with your monthly bills, interest charges will quickly add up. Going into debt because of credit card bills is the surest sign of a low financial IQ.

B **Express Your Ideas.** Which tip do you think is the most important one to follow? Why? Can you think of any others?

C 🎧 **Sound Bites.** Read and listen to a conversation between two friends about saving money.

DAVID: Hey, a new entertainment system! What did you do—strike it rich?
JUDY: I wish! No, I saved up for it.
DAVID: There's no way I could do that. Too many bills.
JUDY: I know what you mean. My credit card bills used to be totally out of hand.
DAVID: Really? Then how did you manage to save up all that cash?
JUDY: Well, I just decided it was time to start living within my means. I cut way back on my spending.
DAVID: Wasn't that hard?
JUDY: Kind of. But I'm glad I did it.

a "piggy bank"

D **Think and Explain.** With a partner, discuss the questions and support your answers with information from Sound Bites.

1. Do you think Judy makes a lot of money?
2. Do you think David is good with money?
3. What was Judy's financial situation like in the past?
4. What did Judy do to change her financial situation?
5. How would you describe Judy's financial IQ?
6. Are you more like Judy or David?

STARTING **POINT**

A **Frame Your Ideas.** What's *your* financial IQ? Choose the statements that best apply to you.

1.	☐ I live within my means.	☐ I live beyond my means.
2.	☐ I keep track of my expenses.	☐ I don't know where the money goes.
3.	☐ I regularly put something away into savings.	☐ I spend everything I have and never save.
4.	☐ I always try to pay my credit card bills in full.	☐ I don't worry about paying my credit card bills off every month.
5.	☐ I always have enough money for what I need.	☐ I can't make ends meet!

B **Pair Work.** Compare your answers with a partner's. Who do you think has the higher financial IQ?

1 GOAL
Talk about your financial goals

Grammar Snapshot. Read the interview responses and notice how future plans are expressed.

What are your short-term and long-term financial goals?

I've decided to set a long-term goal for myself—to put aside enough money to buy a new car. **By this time next year, I'll have put away** enough cash for a down payment. My short-term goal is to start living within my means. **Once I've started** sticking to a monthly budget, I think it'll be easy.

**David Michaels, 24
Brisbane, Australia**

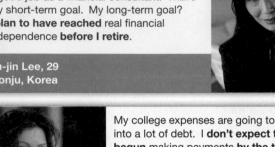

I find it really helps me to try and picture where I want to be over the next few years. **By next year,** I **hope to have gotten** a good job as a financial consultant. That's my short-term goal. My long-term goal? I **plan to have reached** real financial independence **before I retire**.

**Su-jin Lee, 29
Wonju, Korea**

My college expenses are going to get me into a lot of debt. **I don't expect to have begun** making payments **by the time I graduate**, but I do have a plan. After I finish school, my short-term goal is to find a job where I can make some good money and begin a payment plan on my loans. Then, I figure that **by the time I'm thirty, I should have paid** back everything I owe.

**Robin Kraus, 22
Boston, USA**

My long-term goal is **to have saved** enough money to spend a year traveling. **By the time I'm forty,** I'm sure **I'll have saved** enough. **After I've seen** some of the world, I **plan to settle down** and buy a house.

**Andreas Festring, 33
Munich, Germany**

B **Make Personal Comparisons.** Discuss how similar you are to any of the people in the Grammar Snapshot. Do you share any of the goals they mentioned? If not, discuss some of *your* goals.

C **Grammar.** Future plans and finished future actions

Future plans

Express general future plans with <u>expect</u>, <u>hope</u>, <u>intend</u>, or <u>plan</u> and an infinitive.
    We **hope to start** putting some money away.
    I **don't plan to be** financially dependent for the rest of my life.

Use the perfect form of an infinitive to express that an action will or might take place before a specified time in the future.
    By this time next year, I plan **to have saved up** enough cash to buy a new car.
    Her goal is **to have paid off** all her debt in five years.

Finished future actions

Use the future perfect to indicate an action that will be completed by a specified time in the future.
    By next year, I **will have completed** my studies, but I **won't have gotten** married.
    How much **will** you **have saved** by next month?

Use the present perfect in an adverbial clause to distinguish between a completed future action and one that will follow it.
    Once I**'ve completed** my studies, I'll get married.
    I'm going shopping when I**'ve finished** my report.

BE CAREFUL! Don't use the future perfect in the adverbial clause.
    NOT I'm going shopping when I ~~will have finished~~ my report.

> **GRAMMAR BOOSTER**
> ▸ p. G5
> • The future continuous
> • The future perfect continuous

D **Grammar Practice.** Complete the paragraph about Ms. Kemper's future plans. Use expect, hope, intend, or plan and an infinitive form of the verb.

Jessica Kemper _____ business school this semester, and then she
                              (1. complete)
_____ a job in the financial industry. However, Ms. Kemper has a lot of debt
          (2. find)
to repay. She's borrowed some money from her parents and some from the bank, but she
_____ everyone back as soon as she can. She _____ a part-time job to
          (3. pay)   (4. get)
help make ends meet while she's paying off her debt.

E **Grammar Practice.** Complete the paragraph about Mr. Randall's future plans. Use expect, hope, intend, or plan and a perfect form of the infinitive.

Paul Randall has been "drowning in debt," so he's decided to make some changes in his

financial habits. By the end of this month, he _____ a realistic budget that he can
                                                              (1. create)
follow. As a matter of fact, he _____ one of his last credit cards by October.
                                          (2. pay off)
In addition, he _____ putting some money away in savings. If he can stick to his
                        (3. begin)
budget, he _____ most of his debt within the year.
                  (4. pay back)

F **Grammar Practice.** On a separate sheet of paper, use the cues to write sentences with the future perfect.

1. By the end of this month / I / put 10 percent of my paycheck in the bank.
2. By the summer / I / save enough to go to Italy.
3. you / pay off your credit card balance by December?
4. When / they / pay the bill in full?

PRONUNCIATION BOOSTER ▸ p. P3
• Sentence rhythm

NOW YOU CAN *Talk about your financial goals*

A **Notepadding.** Write your short-term and long-term financial goals on your notepad.

IDEAS
• be financially independent
• save enough to buy _____
• cut back on expenses
• create a budget
• pay my debts in full
• live within my means

short-term goals	completion dates	long-term goals	completion dates
buy a new car	by this time next year	buy a house	by the time I'm thirty

short-term goals	completion dates	long-term goals	completion dates

B **Use the Grammar.** Describe your future financial goals to a partner.

"Once I've started working, I plan to put a little something into savings every week."

"By the time I graduate, I hope to have saved enough to buy a new car."

2 GOAL
Express buyer's remorse

A 🎧 1:26 **Conversation Snapshot.** Read and listen. Notice the conversation strategies.

A: **Hey,** I heard you got an E-tec MP3 player. Lucky you!

B: Well, **to tell you the truth,** I could kick myself.

A: **What do you mean?**

B: I had no idea it would be so hard to operate. It took me hours to figure out how to download a song.

A: What a pain!

B: **You're telling me.** Had I known, I would have gotten a different brand.

🎧 1:27 **Rhythm and intonation practice**

B 🎧 1:28 **Vocabulary. Expressing Buyer's Remorse.** Listen and practice.

It costs so much to maintain.

It takes up so much room.

It's so hard to operate.

It's so hard to put together.

It just sits around collecting dust.

C 🎧 1:29 **Listening. Infer Reasons.** Listen to the conversations in which people regret having bought something. Complete each statement by inferring the reason for buyer's remorse.

1. He's sorry he bought it because ....
   a. it costs so much to maintain   **b.** it takes up so much room

2. She's sorry she bought it because ....
   a. it's so hard to operate   **b.** it's so hard to put together

3. She's sorry she bought it because ....
   a. it takes up so much room   **b.** it just sits around collecting dust

4. He's sorry he bought it because ....
   a. it just sits around collecting dust   **b.** it's so hard to put together

5. She's sorry she bought it because ....
   a. it costs so much to maintain   **b.** it's so hard to operate

D Grammar. The past unreal conditional: inverted form

Past unreal conditionals can be stated without if. Invert had and the subject.

If I had known it would take up so much room, I wouldn't have bought it.	→	**Had I known** it would take up so much room, I wouldn't have bought it.
I might have gotten another brand **if I had realized** it would be so hard to operate.	→	I might have gotten another brand **had I realized** it would be so hard to operate.
If we hadn't been so busy, we could have shopped around.	→	**Had we not been** so busy, we could have shopped around.
If I'd been told they wouldn't operate without batteries, I would never have considered getting them.	→	**Had I been told** they wouldn't operate without batteries, I would never have considered getting them.

REMEMBER

Use the past unreal conditional to describe unreal or untrue conditions and results.

E Grammar Practice. On a separate sheet of paper, rewrite the following past unreal conditional sentences, using the inverted form.

1. They would have lent her the money if she had asked.

2. If I had been debt free, I would have considered buying that house.

3. If the Carsons hadn't been able to support their son, he would have had to find a part-time job.

4. Could you have gotten the car if they hadn't raised the price?

F Integrated Practice. Make statements of buyer's remorse, using the inverted form of the past unreal conditional and the Vocabulary. Compare statements with a partner.

1. . . . I would never have gotten that espresso maker.

2. . . . we never would have bought such a large sofa.

3. . . . I could have gotten an entertainment center with fewer pieces.

4. . . . we probably would have bought a more economical car.

5. . . . I would have gotten a DVD player with simpler directions.

*"**Had I known** it would take up so much room, I would never have gotten that espresso maker."*

NOW YOU CAN *Express buyer's remorse*

A Notepadding. On your notepad, answer the questions about something *you* regret buying. Tell your partner about it.

B Use the Conversation Strategies. Role-play a conversation about the item on your notepad. Use the Conversation Snapshot as a guide. Start like this: "Hey, I heard you got . . . ."

> What did you buy?
>
> Why did you buy it?
>
> Do you still have it?
>
> If so, where is it?
>
> If not, what did you do with it?
>
> Would you ever buy a similar item again?
>
> Why or why not?

31

3

Describe your spending habits

A 🎧 **Listening. Listen for Main Ideas.** Read the statements. Then listen to a radio call-in show and check <u>True</u> or <u>False</u>.

	True	False
1. Steve finds it hard to save money.	☐	☐
2. Steve buys a lot on credit.	☐	☐
3. Steve spends less money than he makes.	☐	☐
4. Steve has been on a budget for three months.	☐	☐

B 🎧 **Listening. Listen for Details.** Now listen again. What are the three tips Lara Savino gives the caller?

1. _____

2. _____ .

3. _____ .

C **Draw Conclusions.** Discuss the questions.

1. Why do you think Steve has a problem with money?

2. Which tip do you think is the most useful? Why?

"Money Talks" with **Lara Savin**

D 🎧 **Vocabulary. Describing Spending Habits.** Listen and practice.

NOUNS

a big spender someone who likes to spend large amounts of money

a spendthrift someone who spends money carelessly, especially when he or she doesn't have a lot of it

a cheapskate / a tightwad someone who does not like spending money and can be unpleasant about it

ADJECTIVES

generous willing to give more money, time, etc., than is expected

cheap / stingy unwilling to spend or give money, even when one has a lot of it

thrifty / frugal using money carefully and wisely

E **Vocabulary Practice.** Complete the sentences about people's spending habits.

1. Can you believe what _____ Martin is! He refused to leave a tip for the waiter!

2. Our grandmother donates to many organizations. She's always been very _____ with her money.

3. He's so _____ that he wouldn't even lend his own son money.

4. George must be wealthy. He's such _____. He always insists on treating his friends to dinner.

5. If you try to be more _____ with your money, you'll have enough when you really need it.

6. Unless you stop being such _____, you're going to get deeper in debt.

A **Frame Your Ideas.** First circle the letter that best completes the statement for you. Then compare your answers with a partner's. Find out if your spending habits are the same or different.

Spending Habits Self-Test

1. You hear a great new song on the radio. You . . .

A. buy the CD at the first store you find it in.
B. shop around until you find the CD on sale.
C. borrow it from a friend.
D. other: ....

2. You'd love a state-of-the-art big-screen TV but you just don't have the money right now. You . . .

A. use your credit card and hope you get a raise this year.
B. cut back on other expenses until you've saved enough.
C. wait until big-screen TVs come down in price.
D. other: ....

3. You have lunch with your two best friends. Your meal was cheaper than theirs. When the bill comes, you . . .

A. offer to pay the entire bill.
B. suggest splitting the bill equally.
C. pay only what you owe.
D. other: ....

4. You're invited to a wedding. You . . .

A. spend more on a gift than you can afford.
B. spend as little on a gift as you can.
C. don't go so you don't have to buy a gift.
D. other: ....

5. You discover a hole in your favorite jacket. You . . .

A. go out and buy a new jacket.
B. have the jacket repaired.
C. wear the jacket—it's no big deal.
D. other: ....

Count up your score.

If you circled three or more As:
You can be generous at times, but you're a bit of a spendthrift. Your motto is "Easy come, easy go!"

If you circled three or more Bs:
You're usually very careful with your money—even thrifty. Your motto is "Everything in moderation."

If you circled three or more Cs:
You hate spending money. Some might say you're a tightwad. Your motto is "Money doesn't grow on trees!"

If you circled three or more Ds:
How would *you* describe your spending habits?

B **Group Work.** Tell your classmates about your spending habits or your partner's. Use the Self-Test and the Vocabulary from page 32.

C **Summarize.** On a separate sheet of paper, describe your spending habits.

I make a good living, but I have trouble sticking to a budget and

4 GOAL
Discuss reasons for charitable giving

A 🎧 **Vocabulary. Charity and Investment.** Listen and practice.

1:33

char·i·ty /ˈtʃærəti/ *n. plural* **charities 1** [C] an organization that gives money, goods, or help to people who are poor, sick etc. **2** [U] charity organizations in general

con·tri·bu·tion /ˌkɑntrəˈbyuʃən/ *n.* **1** [C] something that you give or do in order to help something be successful **2** [C] an amount of money that you give in order to help pay for something

in·vest·ment /ɪnˈvɛstmənt/ *n.* **1** [C,U] the money that people or organizations have put into a company, business, or bank, in order to get a profit or to make a business activity successful **2** [C,U] a large amount of time, energy, emotion etc. that you spend on something

phi·lan·thro·pist /fɪˈlænθrəpɪst/ *n.* [C] a rich person who gives money to help people who are poor or who need money to do useful things

pro·fit /ˈprɑfɪt/ *n.* [C,U] money that you gain by selling things or doing business

Excerpted from *Longman Advanced American Dictionary* © 2007

B **Reading Warm-up.** What are some reasons people donate money? What kinds of people or organizations get contributions? Why?

C 🎧 **Reading.** Read the article. What reasons does Paul Newman give for donating to charity?

1:34

On your ActiveBook disc: *Reading Glossary* and *Extra Reading Comprehension Questions*

Paul Newman: Actor and Philanthropist

Actor Paul Newman began acting in 1954 and appeared in more than fifty films in his lifetime. He won an Oscar for best actor in 1986 for *The Color of Money*. In 1993, Newman received a special Oscar for humanitarian service. These two awards reflect his dual success as actor and philanthropist.

In 1982, Newman and a friend, A.E. Hotchner, founded Newman's Own, a not-for-profit food products company. The company's first product was a salad dressing that Newman and Hotchner made at home themselves. Newman was told that the salad dressing would sell only if his face were on the label. Though he didn't want to call attention to himself, Newman agreed because he planned to donate all profits to charity. The salad dressing was a big success: In the first year, Newman contributed approximately US$1,000,000 to charitable organizations.

Newman's Own expanded, and the company now makes many other food products. Every year, Newman donated 100% of the profits from the sale of Newman's Own products to thousands of educational and charitable organizations. And since Paul Newman's death in 2008, Newman's Own, Inc. continues this practice and has donated more than US $295 million to charities in the U.S. and 31 other countries around the world.

One of Newman's special projects was the Hole in the Wall Gang Camps, the world's only network of camps for children with life-threatening illnesses. At these camps, children participate in many outdoor activities where they can temporarily forget their illnesses. Newman and other generous donors have sponsored over 100,000 children to attend these camps free of charge. When asked why he gave so much to children with illnesses, Newman said, "I've had such a string of good fortune in my life…. Those who are most lucky should hold their hands out to those who aren't."

Paul Newman didn't think that being philanthropic was an exceptional quality. To him, generosity was simply a human trait, a common-sense way of living. "I respect generosity in people. I don't look at it as philanthropy. I see it as an investment in the community. I am not a professional philanthropist," said Newman. "I'm not running for sainthood. I just happen to think that in life we need to be a little like the farmer who puts back into the soil what he takes out."

"I don't look at it as philanthropy. I see it as an investment in the community."

Information source: www.newmansown.com

D **Express and Support an Opinion.** Discuss the questions.

1. Why do you think Paul Newman's face has helped to sell his products?

2. Do you think that the work Newman is doing is making a difference?

3. In your opinion, do famous or wealthy people have a responsibility to "give back" or to share what they have with others?

NOW YOU CAN *Discuss reasons for charitable giving*

A **Pair Work.** Read the list of possible reasons some people donate money. In your opinion, which are good reasons? Explain.

- to change society
- to feel good about themselves
- to get publicity or advertising
- to say "thank you" for past help
- to share what they have with others

- to give new opportunities to people
- to satisfy religious beliefs
- so other people will thank them
- so other people will admire them
- other: ....

B **Notepadding.** On your notepad, check the people or organizations you might consider making a contribution to. List your reasons for giving or *not* giving.

People / Organizations	Reasons for giving or *not* giving
☐ a homeless person	
☐ a seriously ill person	
☐ a political candidate	
☐ a disaster relief agency	
☐ a hospital	
☐ a school in a poor neighborhood	
☐ a theater or a museum	
☐ a local charity	
☐ an international charity	
☐ a religious institution	
☐ other:	

C **Discussion.** Talk about the people and organizations you would or would not give money to. Use your notepad. Explain your reasons.

> *"I would rather give money to a local charity because they'll use it to help people in my community."*

D **Presentation.** Choose one person, charity, or type of organization people donate money to. Write a paragraph explaining the reasons why people should donate to this cause. Use the Vocabulary from page 34 in your paragraph. Then present your ideas to your class or group.

Writing: Explain your financial goals

Sequencing Events: Review

When writing a paragraph, the sentences need to be logically organized. **Time order words** are used to clarify the order of events in someone's life, to present the steps in a process, or to give instructions.

Special time order words and expressions help make sequence clear:

- First,
  First of all,
  To begin with,

- Second,
  Third,

- Next,
  Then,
  Following that,

- After,
  Afterwards,
  After that,

- Finally,
  Lastly,
  In the end,

WRITING MODEL

I intend to be financially independent by the time I am sixty. How? **To begin with,** I plan to live within my means. I will cut corners where I can and stick to my budget. **Then,** I hope to open up my own business. **Next,** I intend to start putting some money away. **After that,** I plan to make some smart investments. **In the end,** by the time I am sixty, I will have saved up enough to retire and buy a nice weekend house.

Topics
- My long-term financial goals
- The steps I need to take in order to buy ....

A **Prewriting. Listing Ideas.** Choose a topic. Then complete the chart.

Topic: ....

	Goal or step	My plan	Completion date
First,			
Then,			
After that,			
Finally,			

B **Writing.** Write a paragraph, using your notes. Use time order words and expressions to organize the sequence of goals or steps in your paragraph. Remember to write a topic sentence.

C **Self-Check.**

☐ Did you use time order words or expressions in the paragraph?
☐ Does the sequence of events in the paragraph make sense?
☐ Does the topic sentence introduce the topic of the paragraph?

A 🎧 **Listening.** Listen to the conversations about money matters. Then decide which statement best summarizes each conversation. Listen again if necessary.

Conversation 1. .... **Conversation 2.** .... **Conversation 3.** ....

    a. If he'd known it would just sit around collecting dust, he never would have bought it.

    b. He's too much of a spendthrift. He should be more frugal.

    c. He's not a spendthrift. He's just feeling generous.

    d. If he'd known it would be so hard to put together, he never would have bought it.

B Complete the statements with words from the box.

    1. Steve Gold, an assistant to a big executive at World Corp, saved his company a lot of money by purchasing airplane tickets online from a discount travel website. His boss appreciated his being so ....

    2. Bill Gates, founder of the Microsoft Corporation, is not only one of the richest men in the world, but he's also one of the most .... The Gates Foundation donates a minimum of US $1.5 billion each year.

    3. Dan Fielding expected that his .... in the ComTech Corporation would result in a nice .... However, the business failed and Dan lost all of his money.

    4. One of the richest women in history, Hetty Green was also notoriously .... She once refused to light the candles on her birthday cake so she could return them to the store for a refund. Hetty is considered to be history's greatest ....

    5. Andrew Carnegie was a famous .... who gave away over US$350 million to .... His largest .... was for US$56 million dollars, which was used to build over 2,500 free public libraries around the world.

charities
contribution
frugal
generous
investment
philanthropist
profit
stingy
tightwad

C Write a conditional sentence for each regret below. Begin with an inverted form ("Had I ...").

    1. a regret about your financial situation

    ....

    2. a regret about something you bought

    ....

    3. a regret about a relationship

    ....

D Express your future plans and goals. Use the perfect form of an infinitive or the future perfect.

    1. Before the end of today, I plan ....

    2. By next month, I will ....

    3. By the end of this English course, I expect ....

    4. By the end of the year, I intend ....

    5. Within five years, I hope ....

Looking Good

GOALS After Unit 4, you will be able to:

1 Discuss appropriate dress
2 Comment on fashion and style
3 Evaluate ways to change one's appearance
4 Discuss appearance and self-esteem

A **Topic Preview.** These pictures depict concepts of ideal beauty at different times and in different places. Do *you* find any of these fashions attractive?

For centuries in Japan, the geisha defined beauty and grace.

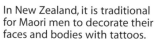

In eighteenth-century Europe, well-to-do men and women wore extravagant wigs and clothing.

Paduang women of Myanmar begin lengthening their necks with gold bands at the age of five or six.

In India, Pakistan, the Middle East, and Africa, women paint their faces and hands with henna for special occasions.

In New Zealand, it is traditional for Maori men to decorate their faces and bodies with tattoos.

B **Express Your Ideas.**

1. What things do people do today to make themselves more attractive? Which techniques do you think are the most successful?

2. In your opinion, why do tastes change over time from culture to culture?

3. What do you think this expression means? Do you agree?

*Beauty is in the eye of the beholder.**

*beholder—the person who is looking

C 🎧 2:02 **Sound Bites.** Read and listen to a conversation between a couple about dressing up and dressing down.

MARGO: Don't you think you might be a little overdressed?

PAUL: What do you mean?

MARGO: Hello! The invitation said casual.

PAUL: Oops. I thought we were supposed to get dressed up. Be right back.

PAUL: How's this?

MARGO: Now that's a little *too* casual.

PAUL: Margo! I wish you'd make up your mind.

MARGO: And what's with the baggy pants?

PAUL: OK. If I change into a polo shirt and a pair of slacks, will that work?

MARGO: Perfect.

D **Activate Language from a Text.** Use the following words to tell the story of what happened in the conversation.

underdressed	overdressed	formal	casual

STARTING **POINT**

A **Apply Ideas.** Look at the pictures. Are the people dressed appropriately for each event? With a partner, use the words from Exercise D to describe how the people are dressed. Then compare your answers with other students'.

B **Relate to Personal Experience.** Discuss the questions.

1. When was the last time you got dressed up? What did you wear?

2. Have you ever been underdressed or overdressed for an event? What happened? How did you feel?

Event: a company picnic

Event: an outdoor wedding

Event: a dinner party at a friend's home

Event: English class

GOAL
Discuss appropriate dress

A 🎧 2:03 **Grammar Snapshot.** Read the article and notice the quantifiers.

Dressing Up for Work

Most professionals around the world wear formal business attire to work in company offices. In **many** countries, there is an unwritten dress code making it mandatory for a man to wear a dark suit and tie and for a woman to wear a skirted suit. But in **several** countries, **more** companies are experimenting with casual business dress during working hours.

Formal business attire: a thing of the past?

In Australia, during the hotter summer months, **a number of** companies are allowing employees to leave their suits at home. And in the United States, **a little over half of all** office workers are allowed to dress down on Fridays. **One third of** U.S. companies make the standard business suit optional—allowing casual clothing **every** day. There is **a great deal of** interest in a casual dress code because of its attraction to new employees.

However, **some** critics complain that casual dress in the office causes **a lot of** problems, among them, **less** productivity. **Each** manager needs to decide if "business casual" is right for his or her company. **A few** experts in the fashion industry claim that the trend toward casual office dress is on the way out. But a recent survey found that **a majority of** employees say their company dress code is at least as casual or more casual than it was two years ago.

Some complain that business casual leads to less productivity.

B **Examine Cultural Expectations.** Discuss the questions.

1. How do professionals dress for work in your country? Do people ever wear "business casual"? What kinds of clothing are mandatory?

2. Do you think the way a person dresses has an effect on how he or she works? In what way?

C **Grammar. Quantifiers**

Some quantifiers can only be used with singular count nouns.

one person	**each** manager	**every** employee

Some quantifiers can only be used with plural count nouns.

two problems	**a couple of** employees	**both** companies
a few managers	**a number of** businesses	**several** women
many young people	**a majority of** professionals	

Some quantifiers can only be used with non-count nouns.

a little conformity	**much** choice	**a great deal of** interest
less productivity	**not as much** satisfaction	

Some quantifiers can be used with *both* count and non-count nouns.

no people	**no** choice
some / any employees	**some / any** conformity
a lot of / lots of companies	**a lot of / lots of** individuality
a third of the companies	**a third of** the money
plenty of businesses	**plenty of** satisfaction
most managers	**most** dissatisfaction
all young people	**all** innovation
more countries	**more** interest

> **NOTE:** The quantifier <u>a majority of</u> can also be used with singular count nouns that include more than one person. Use a third-person singular verb.
> A majority of **the class thinks** business casual is a good idea.
> A majority of **the population prefers** a strict dress code.

GRAMMAR BOOSTER
▶ p. G6

- Quantifiers: review
- <u>A few</u> and <u>few</u>, <u>a little</u> and <u>little</u>
- Using <u>of</u>
- Used without referents
- Subject-verb agreement with quantifiers with <u>of</u>

D Grammar Practice. Circle the correct quantifier. Explain your answer.

"*Businesspeople* is a plural count noun."

1. (Most / Much) businesspeople today prefer to dress casually.

2. (A number of / A great deal of) companies would prefer not to change their dress codes.

3. (All / Every) manager has to decide what is best for the company and its employees.

4. (One / Several) company in New Zealand decided to try a "casual summer" because the summers are always so hot.

5. Research has shown that a business casual dress code has resulted in (less / a few) job dissatisfaction among professionals.

6. (A little / A few) companies are returning to a more formal dress code.

E Grammar Practice. Read the Grammar Snapshot again. On a separate sheet of paper, rewrite the article, using different quantifiers with similar meanings.

Most professionals around the world wear formal business attire to work in company offices.

A majority of professionals around the world wear formal business attire to work in company offices.

F 🎧 2:04 Listening. Infer Information. Listen to the conversations about casual and formal dress. Determine how best to complete each statement.

1. He'd prefer to ....   **a.** dress up   **b.** dress down

2. She wants to ....   **a.** dress up   **b.** dress down

3. He's pretty sure a tie is ....   **a.** optional   **b.** mandatory

4. She thinks a dress is ....   **a.** optional   **b.** mandatory

NOW YOU CAN *Discuss appropriate dress*

A Frame Your Ideas. How do you think people in your country would generally suggest dressing for these events? Discuss appropriate and inappropriate dress for each event.

"*Most people would ...,
but a few people ....*"

Events
- a business meeting
- dinner at a nice restaurant
- dinner at the home of your friend's parents
- an evening party at a club or restaurant with your classmates
- an in-class party

B Use the Grammar. In a group, compare your classmates' opinions. Use quantifiers to summarize your classmates' ideas.

"*A majority of* the class said ...."

"*A few* students said ...."

C Discussion.

1. Do you think it's important to dress according to social conventions? Explain.
2. How does what people wear affect how others perceive them?

2 GOAL
Comment on fashion and style

A 🎧 2:05 **Conversation Snapshot.** Read and listen. Notice the conversation strategies.

A: Check out that guy over there.

B: Which guy?

A: The one on the cell phone. **Can you believe** what he's wearing?

B: What do you mean?

A: **Don't you think** that shirt's a little flashy?

B: **Well,** the colors **ARE** pretty loud, but that's what's in style.

🎧 2:06 **Rhythm and intonation practice**

B 🎧 2:07 **Vocabulary. Describing Fashion and Style.** Listen and practice.

Attractive

fashionable / stylish · modern
in style / trendy / hot* · temporarily popular
elegant / chic · in good taste
striking · attention-getting

Unattractive

old-fashioned / out of style · no longer popular
tacky* · in poor taste
flashy* · attention-getting
shocking · offensive

*informal

PRONUNCIATION BOOSTER ▸ p. P3
• Linking sounds

C 🎧 2:08 **Listening. Listen to Activate Vocabulary.** Listen to the conversations about fashion and style. Choose the adjective from the Vocabulary that best summarizes each speaker's point of view.

1. They think the purses in the magazine are ....
   a. hot   **b.** flashy   **c.** elegant

2. He thinks the jacket Carl is wearing is ....
   a. stylish   **b.** flashy   **c.** striking

3. They think the girl's hairstyle is ....
   a. striking   **b.** old-fashioned   **c.** shocking

4. He thinks the dress the salesperson is suggesting is ....
   a. elegant   **b.** striking   **c.** trendy

5. She thinks the blouse her friend's holding is ....
   a. out of style   **b.** tacky   **c.** chic

42 UNIT 4

D **Vocabulary Practice.** What do you and your partner think of these fashions and hairstyles? Use the adjectives from the Vocabulary to describe them in your *own* way.

E **Think and Explain.** With a partner, read and match each quote with a person in the photos in Exercise D. Explain your answers. Which quote sounds the most like *you*?

1. ○ *"Clothing should express your individuality. I don't want to conform to how other people look or what they wear—I prefer to stand out in a crowd."*

2. ○ *"What I wear may not be the most trendy— but I like it that way. I'd rather be comfortable than fashionable."*

3. ○ *"The way you dress affects how people perceive you, so it's important to dress well. I always choose designer labels—they're the best."*

4. ○ *"I draw the line at wild and crazy clothes. I just don't like to attract attention to myself. I'm a lot more comfortable in subdued colors and classic styles."*

5. ○ *"I prefer a look that isn't just a fad that won't be in style for very long. I prefer clothes that are well made—they may cost a bit more, but they last longer."*

NOW YOU CAN *Comment on fashion and style*

A **Frame Your Ideas.** Complete each statement about fashions in your *own* way. Use these words and expressions.

I prefer clothes that . . .
I don't like to . . .
I dislike it when women wear clothes that . . .
I dislike it when men wear clothes that . . .

conform
stand out
attract attention
express one's
  individuality

old-fashioned
out of style
tacky
flashy
shocking

well made
comfortable
wild and crazy
classic
subdued
fashionable
stylish
elegant
striking
trendy

B **Use the Conversation Strategies.** Explain why you find some fashions attractive and some unattractive. Refer to the photos on this page or bring in others. Use the Vocabulary from page 42 and the Conversation Snapshot as a guide. Start with one of the following expressions:

"Check out . . ."   *"Can you believe . . ."*

GOAL
Evaluate ways to change one's appearance

A 🎧 **Listening. Infer Information.** Listen to Part 1 of a radio program about men's hairstyles. Then read the statements and listen again. Complete the statements, according to the information in the program.

2:09

a goatee

1. In the eighteenth century, wigs were considered ....
   a. chic   **b.** tacky   **c.** out of style

2. In the nineteenth century, wigs were considered ....
   a. in style   **b.** old-fashioned   **c.** striking

3. Before the twentieth century, short hair would not have been considered ....
   a. stylish   **b.** out of style   **c.** shocking

B 🎧 **Listening. Listen to Summarize.** Now listen to Part 2. What generally happened to men's hairstyles in the mid-twentieth century?

2:10

C 🎧 **Listening. Infer Information.** Read the following statements and listen to Part 2 again. Complete the statements, according to the information in the program.

2:11

1. Men changed their hairstyles in the 1960s as a .... statement.
   a. fashion   **b.** social and political   **c.** religious and moral

2. Twenty years ago, the bald look would have been considered ....
   a. eccentric   **b.** stylish   **c.** old-fashioned

3. Young people who dye their hair want to ....
   a. be stylish   **b.** conform   **c.** express their individuality

D **Express and Support an Opinion.** Do you agree with the hair stylist that "anything goes" today for men's hairstyles? Are there any hairstyles that you really don't like on a man? Do you think men's hairstyles have improved or gotten worse in recent times?

sideburns

highlights

long hair

a buzz cut

bald

dyed

braids

A Frame Your Ideas. Discuss and complete the checklist with a partner.

Ways people spend time and money to make themselves more attractive

Which do you think are good ideas for women? How about for men? Which do you think are good for both? Check the appropriate box.

	men	women		men	women
skin lightening	☐	☐	contact lenses	☐	☐
skin tanning	☐	☐	false eyelashes	☐	☐
body piercing	☐	☐	makeup	☐	☐
tattoos	☐	☐	hair coloring	☐	☐
facials	☐	☐	permanents (perms)	☐	☐
manicures	☐	☐	hair transplants	☐	☐
nail extensions	☐	☐	wigs	☐	☐
nail polishing	☐	☐	hair removal	☐	☐
cosmetic surgery	☐	☐	other	☐	☐

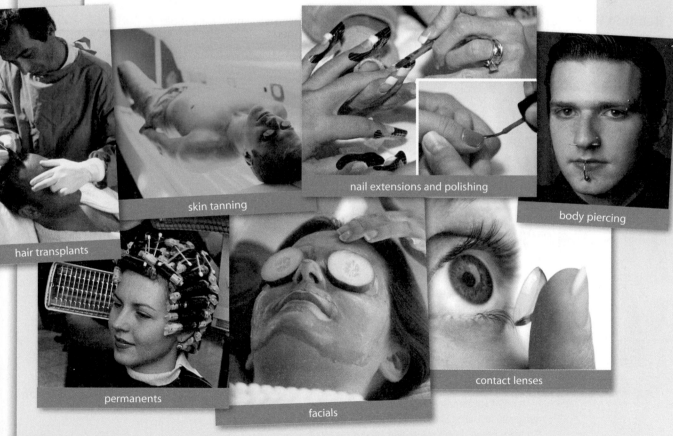

hair transplants

skin tanning

nail extensions and polishing

body piercing

permanents

facials

contact lenses

B Discussion.

1. Who do you think should spend more time making themselves attractive—men or women? Why?

2. Can people do too much to try to make themselves attractive? If so, what do you think is "too much"?

45

4 | GOAL
Discuss appearance and self-esteem

A 🎧 2:12 **Word Skills. Using the Prefix Self-.** Use a dictionary to find other words with the prefix self-.

NOUNS

self-confidence the belief that one has the ability to do things well
Parents can build their children's self-confidence by praising their accomplishments.

self-esteem the attitude of acceptance and approval of oneself
High self-esteem can help a person succeed, and low self-esteem can be damaging.

self-image the opinion one has about one's own abilities, appearance, and character
Mark's self-image improved after he started his new job.

self-pity the feeling of being sorry for oneself
It's easy to indulge in self-pity when you're faced with problems.

ADJECTIVES

self-centered interested only in oneself
Children are naturally self-centered, but they usually learn to be more interested in others as they grow up.

self-confident sure of oneself; not shy or nervous in social situations
Janet is a very self-confident young woman. She'll do well at the university.

self-conscious worried about what one looks like or what other people think of one's appearance
Everyone at the meeting was dressed casually, so I felt self-conscious in my suit.

self-critical tending to find fault with oneself
Paul is too self-critical. He always focuses on his mistakes rather than his accomplishments.

B **Reading Warm-up.** Do you think most people are self-conscious about how they look?

C 🎧 2:13 **Reading.** Read the article about female body image. What do you think is expressed in the song lyrics?

The average fashion model is 5 feet, 11 inches (1.83 meters) tall and weighs 117 pounds (53 kilograms). The average woman is 5 feet, 4 inches (1.65 meters) tall and weighs 140 pounds (63.5 kilograms).

WHO DEFINES BEAUTY?

"Am I not pretty enough?
Is my heart too broken?
. . .
Why do you see right through me?"

What makes a girl beautiful? The lines above are from the song "Not Pretty Enough," written and performed by Kasey Chambers, an Australian folk-rock singer and songwriter. The words tell us a lot about what it's like to be female in a society in which media such as television, movies, and magazines define what it means to be beautiful.

In cultures where success and happiness are equated with being thin and attractive "just like models or movie stars," many young women are left feeling either invisible or fat and unaccepted.

It might not surprise you to read that 75 percent of women in the United States think that they are "too fat." But many people do not realize how these ideas about body image have affected teenagers and children. You don't have to look much farther than a billboard sign, magazine advertisement, or popular television show to see how girls and women are being presented and to understand how it affects them.

On average, U.S. children age eight or older spend almost seven hours a day watching television, playing video games, or reading magazines. Studies have revealed these trends:

- If they had just one wish, girls ages eleven to seventeen say they would wish to be thinner.
- Between the ages of ten and fourteen, the percentage of girls who are "happy with the way I am" drops from 60% to 29%.
- 80% of ten-year-old girls are on diets.
- Between 5 and 10 million teenage girls and young women have an eating disorder—extreme dieting—that can be dangerous to their health.
- Teenage cosmetic surgeries more than doubled in the last decade and are growing at an alarming rate.
- 70% of girls say they have wanted to look like an actress. About 30% have actually tried to.

Young people can benefit from realizing how much they are being targeted as a consumer group and how media messages are used to either sell them products or convey messages about body image, self-esteem, social values, and behavior.

On your ActiveBook disc: **Reading Glossary** and **Extra Reading Comprehension Questions**

Information source: www.riverdeep.net

D **Identify Supporting Details.** Complete each statement, according to "Who Defines Beauty?" Then support your answers, using information from the article.

1. The media can be damaging to young people's ....
   a. self-image **b.** high self-esteem **c.** self-pity

2. If girls had more ...., they would not want to look like fashion models.
   a. self-pity **b.** self-confidence **c.** self-image

3. Before the age of ten, most girls are ....
   a. self-conscious **b.** self-confident **c.** self-critical

4. After the age of ten, a lot of teenage girls suffer from ....
   a. too much self-confidence **b.** high self-esteem **c.** low self-esteem

E **Apply Ideas.** Discuss the questions.

1. Are girls and women in your country affected by images in the media? Are boys and men also affected? How?

2. What do you think young people can do to avoid being affected by the messages they get from advertising, TV, and the movies? What can they do to be more satisfied with the way they look and to develop their self-esteem?

NOW YOU CAN *Discuss appearance and self-esteem*

A **Frame Your Ideas.** Take the survey. Then compare and explain your choices with a partner.

How much do you agree with each statement about men and women in your country?

strongly disagree ← → strongly agree

1. Most women are self-conscious about their bodies.	1	2	3	4	5
2. Most men are self-conscious about their bodies.	1	2	3	4	5
3. Most women are self-conscious about their faces.	1	2	3	4	5
4. Most men are self-conscious about their faces.	1	2	3	4	5
5. Most women want to look more like people in the media.	1	2	3	4	5
6. Most men want to look more like people in the media.	1	2	3	4	5
7. Most women think beauty is not important.	1	2	3	4	5
8. Most men think beauty is not important.	1	2	3	4	5

B **Notepadding.** Make a list of factors that affect self-esteem.

Build self-esteem	Interfere with self-esteem

C **Discussion.**

1. Do you think life is easier for people who are attractive? Why or why not?

2. Do you think people should just accept the way they look or try to change their appearances?

3. In an ideal world, what should one's self-esteem be based on?

Writing: *Compare two people's tastes in fashion*

Compare and Contrast: Review

Compare (show similarities)	Contrast (show differences)
like Like Sylvia, I wear jeans all the time.	**unlike** Unlike her sister, Wendy wears great clothes. OR Wendy wears great clothes, **unlike** her sister.

similarly
I grew up paying little attention to fashion.
  Similarly, Mel was not very interested in clothes.
OR I grew up paying little attention to fashion;
  similarly, Mel was not very interested in clothes.
	in contrast
	I've always liked body piercings and tattoos.
	  In contrast, my boyfriend thinks they're ugly.
	OR I've always liked body piercings and tattoos;
	  in contrast, my boyfriend thinks they're ugly.

likewise
My mother always liked elegant clothes.
  Likewise, her two sisters did too.
OR My mother always liked elegant clothes;
  likewise, her two sisters did too.
	however
	Lily had to wear a uniform when she was in school.
	  However, I was able to wear anything I wanted.
	OR Lily had to wear a uniform when she was in school;
	  however, I was able to wear anything I wanted.

as well / not either
Many people spend too much money on clothes.
  They spend too much on shoes **as well**.
Our parents' generation didn't worry so much
  about fashion. Their own parents **didn't either**.
	whereas / while
	Sam spends a lot of money on clothes, **whereas**
	  Jeff shops in thrift stores.
	OR Sam spends a lot of money on clothes, **while**
	  Jeff shops in thrift stores.

A **Prewriting. Organizing Ideas.**
Choose a topic and draw a diagram similar to the one on the right. Label the circles with the topics you are comparing and write <u>Both</u> in the middle. List the differences in each circle and the similarities in the middle.

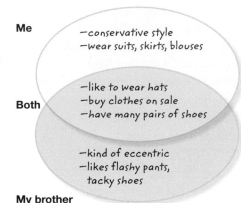

Me
—conservative style
—wear suits, skirts, blouses

Both
—like to wear hats
—buy clothes on sale
—have many pairs of shoes

—kind of eccentric
—likes flashy pants,
  tacky shoes

My brother

Topics
• Compare and contrast your fashion style with that of someone you know.
• Compare and contrast fashion today with fashion five, ten, or twenty years ago.

B **Writing.** Write two paragraphs comparing and contrasting ideas, referring to the notes in your diagram. In your first paragraph, write about the differences. In your second paragraph, write about the similarities. Use connecting words and include a topic sentence for each paragraph.

C **Self-Check.**
☐ Did you correctly use connecting words for comparing?
☐ Did you correctly use connecting words for contrasting?
☐ Does each paragraph have a topic sentence?

Review

ActiveBook: *More Practice*

grammar · vocabulary · listening
reading · speaking · pronunciation

A 🎧 **Listening.** Listen carefully to the conversations about tastes in fashion. Infer which adjective best describes what each person thinks.

1. The man thinks the suit is ....
   a. stylish   **b.** out of style   **c.** tacky

2. The woman thinks the dress is ....
   a. chic   **b.** old-fashioned   **c.** flashy

3. The man thinks the tie is ....
   a. fashionable   **b.** out of style   **c.** shocking

4. The woman thinks the shoes are ....
   a. out of style   **b.** in style   **c.** striking

B Complete each statement with an appropriate word or phrase.

1. A set of rules for how to dress in a particular situation is a dress ....

2. In the United States and Canada, many companies allow their employees to wear "business ...." on Fridays—they don't have to wear suits, skirts, or ties.

3. Some companies allow employees to dress .... for some business meetings where the focus is on getting to know each other in a more casual setting.

4. When a fashion is .... style, people no longer wear that fashion. When a fashion is .... style, everyone wants to wear it.

C Cross out the one quantifier that *cannot* be used in each sentence.

1. (Every / A few / Most) older people find today's fashions pretty shocking.

2. Our company says that it will allow us to dress down (one / a couple of / a few) days a week.

3. (Most / Many / Every) young girls aren't worried about the way they look.

4. (Much / A majority of / A number of) researchers are concerned about the effect the media has on young boys as well.

5. (Many / Most / Much) men wore their hair very short in the 1930s.

6. I'd say your sister could use (some / a little / a few) fashion help.

7. There are (several / most / many) reasons why so many people have eating disorders.

8. A new study says that (most / many / every) children who watch TV for more than six hours a day may have problems with self-esteem as teenagers.

D Write a paragraph explaining your opinion about one of these expressions. Give concrete examples from your life.

"Beauty is only skin-deep."   "Beauty is in the eye of the beholder."

Community

GOALS After Unit 5, you will be able to:

1 Politely ask someone not to do something
2 Complain about public conduct
3 Discuss social responsibility
4 Identify urban problems

A **Topic Preview.** Look at the graph and photos. Where do most people live in your country—in rural or urban areas?

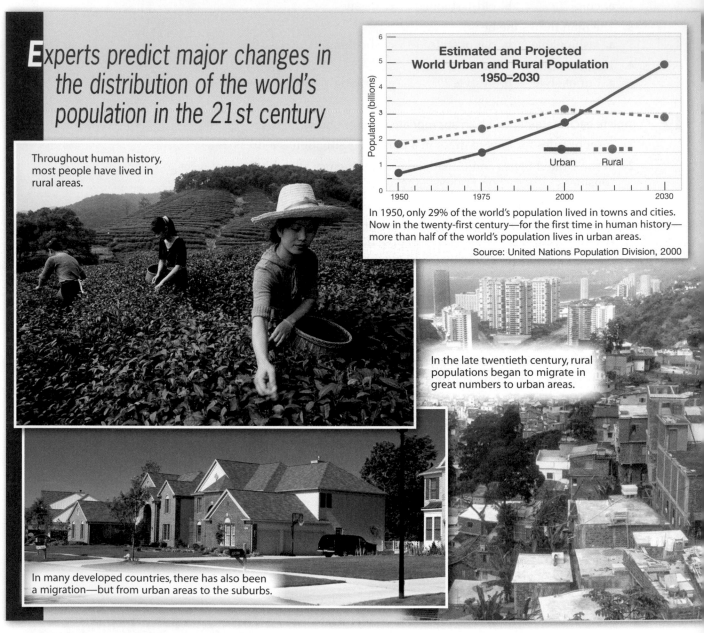

Experts predict major changes in the distribution of the world's population in the 21st century

Throughout human history, most people have lived in rural areas.

Estimated and Projected World Urban and Rural Population 1950–2030

Urban   Rural

In 1950, only 29% of the world's population lived in towns and cities. Now in the twenty-first century—for the first time in human history—more than half of the world's population lives in urban areas.

Source: United Nations Population Division, 2000

In the late twentieth century, rural populations began to migrate in great numbers to urban areas.

In many developed countries, there has also been a migration—but from urban areas to the suburbs.

B **Interpret Data from a Graph.** With a partner, answer the questions, according to the information in the graph.

   1. Approximately how many people in the world will be living in urban areas in 2030? How about in rural areas?

   2. In what year did the world's urban population surpass the world's rural population?

C **Express Your Ideas.** Is there much migration in your country? What are some reasons people migrate?

D 🎧 2:15 **Sound Bites.** Read and listen to a conversation about city life.

DON: Hey, Kyle! So how's the big city treating you?

KYLE: Funny you should ask. Not great.

DON: What do you mean?

KYLE: Well, on my way here, I'm crossing the street and this guy in an SUV turns the corner and almost runs me over.

DON: Are you serious?

KYLE: Yeah. The driver was in such a big hurry he didn't even notice. I just can't keep up with the pace here.

DON: Well, you *do* have to learn to stay on your toes in the city.

KYLE: It really gets to me sometimes. I don't think I'll ever get used to it. I guess I'm just a country boy at heart.

"the city"

E **Think and Explain.** Read the conversation again. With a partner, explain the meaning of each of the following statements or questions.

1. "So how's the big city treating you?"
2. "I just can't keep up with the pace here."
3. "You do have to learn to stay on your toes."
4. "It really gets to me sometimes."
5. "I'm just a country boy at heart."

"the country"

STARTING **POINT**

A **Frame Your Ideas.** What are some advantages and disadvantages of living in each type of place? Write them in the chart.

	Advantages	Disadvantages
the country		
the city		
the suburbs		

B **Discussion.** Where would you prefer to live—in the country, the city, or the suburbs? Why?

1 GOAL
Politely ask someone not to do something

A 🎧 2:16 **Conversation Snapshot.** Read and listen.
Notice the conversation strategies.

A: **Do you mind** my smoking here?

B: **Actually,** smoking kind of bothers me.
I hope that's not a problem.

A: **Not at all.** I can step outside.

B: That's very considerate of you. Thanks
for asking.

> 🎧 2:18 **Ways to soften an objection**
> I hope that's not a problem.
> I hope you don't mind.
> I hope it's OK / all right.
> I don't mean to
> inconvenience you.

🎧 2:17 **Rhythm and intonation practice**

B **Grammar. Possessives with gerunds**

**You can use a possessive before a gerund when you want to indicate the performer
of the action.**

> **The kids' singing** was too loud.
> **Your** constant **arguing** is getting on my nerves.
> I didn't like **their talking** during the movie.
> You should complain about **Sam's cutting** in line.
> The thing that bothers me is **her smoking**.

In informal spoken English, a noun or an object pronoun is often used instead of a possessive.

> I can understand **John being** annoyed. (instead of "John's being annoyed")
> I can't accept **them ignoring** me. (instead of "their ignoring me")

C **Grammar Practice.** Combine the two statements, using a possessive
with a gerund.

Example: They allow smoking. I'm not in favor of it.
I'm not in favor of their allowing smoking.

1. He plays his MP3 player in the library. I don't appreciate that.

2. They smoke cigars in the car. My mother objects to it.

3. She's talking on her cell phone. We don't mind it.

4. My brother litters. I'm really annoyed by it.

D 🎧 2:19 **Word Skills.** Using Negative Prefixes to Form Antonyms.

1. acceptable → **un**acceptable
2. considerate → **in**considerate
3. polite → **im**polite

4. proper → **im**proper
5. respectful → **dis**respectful
6. responsible → **ir**responsible

Negative prefixes
dis-   ir-
im-   un-
in-

PRONUNCIATION BOOSTER ▸ p. P4
• Unstressed syllables

E **Word Skills Practice.** Use a dictionary to find antonyms for the following words. What other adjectives can you find with negative prefixes?

1. appropriate → ....
2. courteous → ....
3. excusable → ....
4. imaginable → ....

5. honest → ....
6. pleasant → ....
7. rational → ....
8. mature → ....

F **Activate Word Skills.** Write your own examples of inappropriate behavior. Use the adjectives from Exercises D and E.

Example: *It's inconsiderate to play loud music on a bus.*

1. ....
2. ....
3. ....
4. ....
5. ....

NOW YOU CAN) *Politely ask someone not to do something*

A **Notepadding.** Discuss situations in which you would probably ask for permission to do something. Make a list on your notepad.

smoking in a restaurant
turning on the TV in a doctor's waiting room
making a call on my cell phone in public

Your list:

B **Use the Conversation Strategies.** Role-play a conversation asking for permission to do something. Your partner politely asks you not to do it. Use the Conversation Snapshot as a guide. Start like this: "Do you mind my . . ."

"Do you mind my smoking?"

"Do you mind my making a quick call on my cell phone?"

53

GOAL
Complain about public conduct

A 🎧 2:20 **Grammar Snapshot.** Read the interview responses and notice the paired conjunctions.

What ticks you off?

**Wendy Kwon, 23
Chicago, USA**

What ticks me off? Well, I can't understand why people litter. Who do they think is going to clean up after them? **Either** they should throw their garbage in a trash can **or** hold on to it till they find one. I think it's great that people have to pay a fine for littering. Maybe they'll think twice before doing it again.

**Dana Fraser, 36
Toronto, Canada**

You know what gets to me? Smoking. It's such an inconsiderate habit. Secondhand cigarette smoke is **neither** good for you **nor** pleasant to be around. I'd like to see smoking banned from more public places. Don't non-smokers have rights too?

**Yuan Yong Jing, 28
Beijing, China**

It really bugs me when people spit on the street. **Not only** do I find it disgusting, **but** it's **also** unhygienic. It's important to think about other people's feelings and public health.

**Jorge Santos, 31
São Paulo, Brazil**

Here's something that gets on my nerves: I hate it when people use their cell phones in public places. They annoy other people, **not only** on trains and buses **but also** in theaters. They should have the courtesy to **either** turn their phones off **or** to leave them at home. It really makes me angry. I guess it's kind of my pet peeve.

B **Express Your Ideas.** Do any of the behaviors described in the interview responses "tick you off"? With a partner, discuss and rate each of them as follows:

| extremely annoying | somewhat annoying | not annoying at all |

GRAMMAR BOOSTER
▶ p. G9

- Conjunctions with so, too, neither, or not either
- So, too, neither, or not either: short responses

C **Grammar. Paired conjunctions**

You can connect related ideas with paired conjunctions.

either . . . or
   Either smoke outside **or** don't smoke at all.
   Cell phones should **either** be turned off **or** left at home.

neither . . . nor
   I would allow **neither** spitting **nor** littering on the street.
   Neither eating **nor** chewing gum is acceptable in class.

not only . . . but (also)
   Not only CD players **but also** cell phones should be banned from trains.

BE CAREFUL! When **not only . . . but (also)** joins two clauses, notice the subject–verb position in the first clause of the sentence.
   Not only **did they forget** to turn off their cell phones, but they also talked loudly during the concert.
   Not only **are they** noisy, but they're rude.

Verb agreement with paired conjunctions

When joining two subjects, make sure the verb agrees with the subject closer to the verb.
   Either the mayor or **local businesspeople need** to decide.
   Either local businesspeople or **the mayor needs** to decide.

D **Grammar Practice.** On a separate sheet of paper, combine the sentences with the paired conjunction indicated. Use <u>or</u>, <u>nor</u>, or <u>but</u> <u>(also)</u>.

1. My uncle isn't willing to give up smoking. My grandparents aren't willing to give up smoking. (neither)

2. People should speak up about what bothers them. They should just learn to live with other people's habits. (either)

3. I don't like it when people use cell phones in theaters. I don't like it when they use them on buses. (not only)

4. The smell of the smoke bothers me. The danger to my health bothers me. (not only)

NOW YOU CAN *Complain about public conduct*

A **Notepadding.** Make a list of some of the things that really get on your nerves in public places. Then write sentences with paired conjunctions to express your opinion. Use some of the adjectives with negative prefixes.

IDEAS
• cutting in line
• graffiti on walls
• talking in theaters
• strong perfumes
• gossiping

In restaurants: *talking on cell phones*
It's not only annoying, but it's also very impolite.

In restaurants:

In stores:

On buses and trains:

On the street:

In offices:

In movie theaters:

Other:

Adjectives with negative prefixes

disrespectful
immature
impolite
inconsiderate
inexcusable
irresponsible
unacceptable
unpleasant

B **Use the Grammar.** One student is an "on-the-street interviewer" and asks the other students about what gets on their nerves. Use the sentences with paired conjunctions from your notepad in your responses.

What really ticks me off is ...

I can't understand why ...

I'll tell you what really gets on my nerves....

You want to know what really bugs me?

C **Discussion.**

1. In your opinion, how should people behave in public places? Do you think it's important to speak up when people behave inconsiderately in public?

2. Do *you* ever do things that annoy other people? Explain.

3 GOAL

Discuss social responsibility

A 🎧 2:21 **Vocabulary. Ways to Perform Community Service.** Listen and practice.

GET INVOLVED WITH YOUR COMMUNITY!

Beautify your town
Plant flowers or trees where there aren't any.

Clean up litter
Pick up trash from parks, playgrounds, or the street.

Donate your time
Mail letters, make phone calls, raise money, or collect signatures for a community service organization.

Volunteer
Work without pay in the fire department, a hospital, or a school.

Donate your organs
Save someone's life by making arrangements <u>now</u> to give your heart, lungs, and other organs after you die to someone who needs them.

B **Vocabulary Practice.** Would you ever consider doing any of the community service activities in the Vocabulary? With a partner, explain why you would or would not.

> *"I would never consider donating my organs because it's against my beliefs."*

C 🎧 2:22 **Listening. Listen to Summarize.** Read the questions and listen to Part 1 of the story about Nicholas Green and his family. Take notes on your notepad. Then summarize the first part of the story with your partner.

Where were the Greens from?
What were they doing in Italy?
What happened to Nicholas?
What decision did his parents make?
How did the Italian people react?

Nicholas Green, age seven, in Switzerland, a few days before he and his family went to Italy

D 🎧 2:23 **Listening. Listen for Details.** Read the questions and listen to Part 2. Discuss your answers with a partner.

1. What changes occurred in Italy after the Greens made their decision? What is "The Nicholas Effect"?

2. How many people received one of Nicholas's organs? What effect did his gift have on their lives?

3. As a result of this incident, what are the Greens doing today?

E **Critical Thinking.** Discuss the questions, using information from the listening passage and your own ideas.

1. Do you think you would have made the same decision the Greens did if you had been in their situation? Why or why not?

2. Why do you think people responded so strongly to this story?

NOW YOU CAN *Discuss social responsibility*

A **Frame Your Ideas.** Consider each situation and discuss what you might do. Based on your answers, how strong do you think your "sense of community" is? Compare ideas with a partner.

"My first responsibility is to my family. I can't imagine doing this for a total stranger."

"I'd be happy to donate money to help a stranger. People should help each other."

1 There has been a terrible storm, and many homes have been destroyed. You're asked to let a family live with you until their home is fixed.

What would you do if they were . . .

    a. your relatives?   c. your colleague's family?

    b. your neighbors?   d. complete strangers?

2 Someone needs a new liver to survive. Doctors say that they can use a piece of your liver to save that person's life.

What would you do if the person were . . .

    a. a family member?   c. your classmate?

    b. your neighbor?   d. a complete stranger?

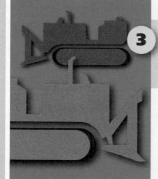

3 Developers plan to destroy a well-known historical monument so they can build a new office building. You're asked to donate your time to help save that monument.

What would you do if the monument were . . .

    a. in your neighborhood?   c. in another city in your country?

    b. in another part of the city?   d. in another country?

B **Discussion.** Have you or someone you know ever volunteered for some kind of community service? How important is it for a person to be active in his or her community? Explain.

GOAL
Identify urban problems

A **Reading Warm-up.** What problems do you think cities of 10 million or more people might share?

B 🎧 2:24 **Reading.** Read the interview. Do you agree with Dr. Perlman's views?

The Advent of the Megacity

Following is an interview with Dr. Janice Perlman, founder and president of Mega-Cities Project, Inc. Her organization attempts to make cities worldwide more livable places by taking good ideas from one place and trying to make them work in another.

Mexico City
over 18 million (2005)

Q. How do you define "megacity"?

A. We define megacities in our work as cities that have reached populations of 10 million or more. The majority of these are in developing countries. Migration to the city is the route for many people to greater choice, opportunity, and well-being. By coming to settle in the city, they have in effect "voted with their feet."

Q. Why are these places going to be very important in the next hundred years?

A. The 21st century won't be a century of rural areas and small towns but of giant cities that will set the standard of how we live, how our environment is preserved (or not preserved), how our economies work, and what kind of civil society we develop.

Tokyo
over 28 million (2005)

Q. Do megacities in the developed and developing world differ, or are they linked by certain similarities?

A. These large cities have a lot more in common with each other than they do with the small towns and villages in their own countries. For example, every megacity struggles with a widening gap between rich and poor. Every "first-world" city, such as Los Angeles, New York, London, or Tokyo, has within it a "third-world" city of poverty and deprivation. And every third-world city, such as Calcutta, Cairo, or Mexico City, has within it a first-world city of high culture, technology, fashion, and finance.

In addition, all megacities share the problems of providing jobs and economic opportunities, and making housing, education, and health care available. They deal with crime and violence, as well as basic infrastructure such as water, sanitation, and public transportation. This is no easy task. The leaders of these cities recognize that they have similar problems, and they would like to learn more from other cities, particularly about successful solutions.

If we are going to create livable cities for the next century, we will need to be clever enough to do it through collaboration and cooperation. That is why the Mega-Cities Project works to share experiences that work across boundaries of culture and geography.

Q. Is the solution to urban problems strict central planning?

A. Absolutely not. We need decentralized planning that includes local citizens. In my view, attempts to create planned cities or communities—like Brasília or Chandigarh—are too sterile and miss the spontaneity of cities that grew organically, like Rio de Janeiro, Bombay, or even New York City. The best example of urban planning I've seen recently is in Curitiba, Brazil, which set up a brilliant public transportation system in anticipation of population growth. The historic areas of cities like Siena, Paris, or Barcelona all have elements of planning that led to buildings of similar heights and architecture, but they were not centrally planned. There is a lot of diversity within the design, and people love to go to those cities.

Megacities are really very exciting places. The truth is, I've never met a megacity that I didn't like!

The World's Ten Largest Urban Areas	Population (millions) in 1996	in 2015	Rank in 2015
1 Tokyo, Japan	27.2	28.9	1
2 Mexico City, Mexico	16.9	19.2	7
3 São Paulo, Brazil	16.8	20.3	4
4 New York, United States	16.4	17.6	9
5 Mumbai (Bombay), India	15.7	26.2	2
6 Shanghai, China	13.7	18	8
7 Los Angeles, United States	12.6	14.2	15
8 Kolkata (Calcutta), India	12.1	17.3	10
9 Buenos Aires, Argentina	11.9	13.9	17
10 Seoul, Korea	11.8	13	19

Source: U.N. Department of Economic and Social Affairs Population Division

On your ActiveBook disc: *Reading Glossary* and *Extra Reading Comprehension Questions*

Information source: www.megacitiesproject.org

C **Confirm Content.** Check the types of urban problems Dr. Perlman mentions or suggests in the interview.

☐ poverty   ☐ pollution   ☐ unemployment   ☐ inadequate public transportation
☐ lack of housing   ☐ disease   ☐ discrimination
☐ crowding   ☐ crime   ☐ corruption

D **Understand from Context.** Read each statement from the interview. Choose the sentence closest to what Dr. Perlman means. Use information from the article to explain your answers.

1. "By coming to settle in the city, they have in effect 'voted with their feet.'"
   a. People are making it clear which kind of life they prefer.
   b. People would rather live in the country than live in the city.
   c. People don't have as much opportunity in the city as they do in the country.

2. "Every 'first-world' city . . . has within it a 'third-world' city of poverty and deprivation. And every third-world city . . . has within it a first-world city of high culture, technology, fashion, and finance."
   a. Some megacities have more poverty than others.
   b. All megacities have both poverty and wealth.
   c. Some megacities have more wealth than others.

3. "The Mega-Cities Project works to share experiences that work across boundaries of culture and geography."
   a. The Mega-Cities Project helps megacities communicate their success stories to the people who live in that city.
   b. The Mega-Cities Project helps megacities communicate their success stories to other cities in that country.
   c. The Mega-Cities Project helps megacities communicate their success stories to megacities in other countries.

E **Infer Information.** Discuss the questions. Support your opinion with information from the article.

1. Why does Dr. Perlman say she prefers cities that are *not* planned over planned cities?
2. Why do you think Dr. Perlman thinks megacities are exciting? Do you agree?
3. Do you live in a megacity, or have you ever visited one? What are the pros and cons of living in a megacity?
4. Do you think life in megacities will improve in the future or get worse? Why?

NOW YOU CAN   *Identify urban problems*

A **Frame Your Ideas.** Check which urban problems you think exist in your area. Discuss with a partner and provide examples.

B **Discussion.** Talk about the problems you've identified. As a group, discuss at least five ways to make improvements in your town or city.

◯ poverty   ◯ pollution
◯ crime   ◯ corruption
◯ crowding   ◯ lack of housing
◯ disease   ◯ discrimination
◯ inadequate public transportation   ◯ unemployment
◯ other: _____

C **Project.** Choose several social problems that exist in your town or city. Write letters to a local newspaper suggesting possible solutions.

Writing: Complain about a problem

Formal Letters: Review

When writing to a friend or family member, an informal tone, casual language, and abbreviations are acceptable. However, when writing to the head of a company, a boss, or someone you don't know, standard formal language should be used, and regular spelling and punctuation rules apply. Formal letters are usually typewritten, not handwritten. The following salutations and closings are appropriate for formal letters:

Formal salutations	Formal closings
Dear Mr. / Mrs. / Ms. / Dr. / Professor [Lee]:	Sincerely (yours),
Dear Sir or Madam:	Respectfully (yours),
To whom it may concern:	Best regards,
	Cordially,

Letters of Complaint

When writing a formal letter of complaint, first state the reason why you are writing and the problem. Then inform whomever you are writing what you would like him or her to do about it, or what *you* plan to do.

WRITING MODEL

your address —[4719 McPherson Avenue
Philadelphia, Pennsylvania 19102

date —[June 30, 2006

Red Maple Café
708 West Pine Street   }— recipient's address
Philadelphia, Pennsylvania 19102

salutation —[Dear Sir or Madam:

I live a few blocks from your restaurant. For the past several months, I have noticed that in the evenings there is a lot of trash on the side of your building. Cats in the neighborhood turn over the garbage cans, and the trash goes everywhere. This is not only unpleasant to look at, but it is also a health hazard.

Could you please make sure that when the trash is put out, the garbage cans are closed? Your helping keep our neighborhood clean and beautiful would be greatly appreciated.

closing —[Respectfully,

Olivia Krum }— signature

Olivia Krum

A **Prewriting. Listing Ideas.** Think of a problem in your community that you would like to complain about. List the reasons why it is a problem.

> Problem: *trash on side of building*
> Reasons: *—unpleasant to look at*
> *—health hazard*

Problem:
Reasons:

B **Writing.** On a separate sheet of paper, use your notes to write a letter of complaint. State what you intend to do or what you would like to see done. Remember to use the appropriate level of formality.

C **Self-Check.**

☐ Did you use the proper salutation and closing?

☐ Are the tone and language in the letter appropriate for the audience?

☐ Did you use regular spelling and punctuation and avoid abbreviations?

D **Peer Response.** Exchange letters with a partner. Write an appropriate response to your partner's letter, as if you were the person to whom it was addressed.

A 🎧 **Listening.** Listen carefully to the conversations about cities. Check the adjectives that are closest in meaning to what the people say about each place. Listen again if necessary.

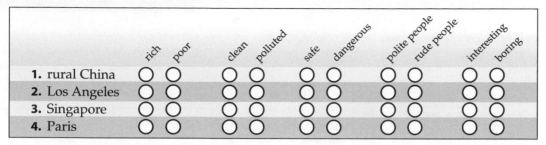

	rich	poor	clean	polluted	safe	dangerous	polite people	rude people	interesting	boring
1. rural China	○	○	○	○	○	○	○	○	○	○
2. Los Angeles	○	○	○	○	○	○	○	○	○	○
3. Singapore	○	○	○	○	○	○	○	○	○	○
4. Paris	○	○	○	○	○	○	○	○	○	○

B Respond to each question in your *own* way.

1. "Do you mind if I call someone on my cell phone?"

   YOU ....

2. "Would you mind not smoking in here?"

   YOU ....

3. "What bugs you about living in your town?"

   YOU ....

4. "Who do you know that really gets on your nerves?"

   YOU ....

C Make each sentence logical by attaching a negative prefix to one of the adjectives. Use a dictionary if necessary.

1. Painting graffiti on public buses and trains is really excusable.

2. I believe littering and spitting on the street are responsible behaviors.

3. Young people who play loud music without consideration for the people around them are exhibiting really proper behavior.

4. I think it's very appropriate for people to scream into their cell phones in theaters.

5. When a salesperson is rude, I find it not only respectful but also annoying.

6. I should warn you that the air pollution downtown is really pleasant.

7. I think politicians who are honest and corrupt should be punished.

8. It doesn't help when people are courteous to each other.

D Combine the sentences with the paired conjunction indicated. Use <u>or, nor,</u> or <u>but (also)</u>.

1. Restaurants shouldn't allow smoking. Theaters shouldn't allow smoking. (neither)

   ....

2. Smoking should be banned. It should be restricted. (either)

   ....

3. Littering doesn't offend me. Spitting doesn't offend me. (neither)

   ....

4. I think loud music is rude. I think loud people are rude. (not only)

   ....

Animals

GOALS After Unit 6, you will be able to:

1 Exchange opinions about the treatment of animals
2 Discuss the benefits of certain pets
3 Compare animal characters
4 Debate the value of animal conservation

A **Topic Preview.** Find your birth year on the Chinese Zodiac. What's your animal sign?

TIGER

1950 1962 1974
1986 1998 2010

Self-confident, independent, and emotional. Sometimes you tend to be inconsiderate and selfish.

RABBIT

1951 1963 1975
1987 1999 2011

Intelligent, kind, and helpful. You are also traditional and somewhat conservative. You tend to tell people what's on your mind.

OX

1949 1961 1973
1985 1997 2009

Hardworking, serious, and responsible. You can sometimes be a workaholic. It's difficult to get you to change your opinions and beliefs, and you get angry easily.

DRAGON

1952 1964 1976
1988 2000 2012

Fun loving, artistic, and truthful. You don't always feel confident in yourself or your abilities. You are also a little eccentric at times.

RAT

1948 1960 1972
1984 1996 2008

Generous, honest, and imaginative. You are usually careful, and sometimes you are a perfectionist.

SNAKE

1953 1965 1977
1989 2001 2013

Attractive and very calm. You are able to make good decisions and give good advice. Sometimes you can be self-centered.

BOAR

1959 1971 1983
1995 2007 2019

Generally quiet and honest. You work hard toward your goals. You don't have many friends, but you are very considerate to the friends you have.

HORSE

1954 1966 1978
1990 2002 2014

Popular, outgoing, and cheerful. You are a real people person. Sometimes you are too talkative.

DOG

1958 1970 1982
1994 2006 2018

Honest, caring, and modest. You are always there for your friends. You may at times seem cold and unfriendly to people who don't know you.

GOAT

1955 1967 1979
1991 2003 2015

Passionate, very artistic, and a bit shy. You are good at understanding other people's problems. Sometimes you are too willing to believe what other people say.

MONKEY

1956 1968 1980
1992 2004 2016

Clever and likable. You have new and interesting ideas, and you learn very quickly. Sometimes you can also be a little egotistical.

ROOSTER

1957 1969 1981
1993 2005 2017

Attractive and self-confident. You want to be very successful. Sometimes you say things just to make people look up to you.

Information source: silverdragonstudio.com

B **Express Your Ideas.**

1. How well do the adjectives for your sign describe your personality? How are you different from the description?

2. Do you think the descriptions match the animals in any way? Why or why not?

C 🎧 2:26 **Sound Bites.** Read and listen to a conversation between two friends at the zoo.

ALICIA: I can't believe I let you talk me into coming here. I really have a problem with zoos.

BEN: C'mon. These guys have got it made. They're well-cared for. They're healthy. They've got plenty of food.

ALICIA: You could say the same thing about people in prisons. What about freedom? I hate seeing animals cooped up in cages.

BEN: You think animals are any happier in the wild? Always hungry? Running from some bigger animal that's trying to eat them?

ALICIA: I don't know. Maybe not.

BEN: Just look at that tiger over there. Where else could you see such a beautiful animal up close?

ALICIA: You're right about that. He *is* magnificent.

D **Think and Explain.** With a partner, discuss the questions and support your answers with information from Sound Bites.

1. What is Alicia's objection to zoos?
2. How is Ben's attitude different from Alicia's?
3. What does Ben mean when he says, "These guys have got it made"?
4. What do Alicia and Ben agree on about zoos?

STARTING POINT

Associate Ideas. What adjectives do you associate with different animals? With a partner, choose five adjectives and discuss an animal you think each adjective describes.

frightening
unusual
fun
friendly
calm
irritating
attractive
loving
unfriendly
independent
disgusting
hardworking
quiet

ADJECTIVE	ANIMAL
1.	
2.	
3.	
4.	
5.	

GOAL
Debate the value of animal conservation

A **Reading Warm-up.** What are some endangered animals you can think of? What are some threats to their survival?

B 🎧 2:36 **Reading.** Read the article. Do you agree with the point of view expressed?

On your ActiveBook disc: *Reading Glossary* and *Extra Reading Comprehension Questions*

Protecting Our Natural Inheritance

The earth is rich in biodiversity with millions of different species of plants and animals. However, many species are disappearing at an alarming rate. Biodiversity is reduced when ecosystems are modified and habitats of plants and animals are destroyed. The one species that is causing this phenomenon is the same one that can stop it—humans.

Many scientists view the current wave of species extinctions as unrivaled since the disappearance of the dinosaurs, more than 65 million years ago. Currently, around 11,000 species of plants and animals are at risk of disappearing forever—this includes over 180 mammals.

There are only about 700 mountain gorillas left in the wild.

Many species cling to survival. Found only in China, the giant panda's habitat has been decimated—the old-growth bamboo forests where the pandas make their home are being destroyed rapidly. It is estimated that as few as 1,600 giant pandas remain in the wild today. In the Arctic, the polar bear's icy habitat is disappearing as a result of global warming, and its survival is at risk. And in Central and East Africa, which have endured decades of civil war, the mountain gorilla population now totals just over 700 individuals.

If present trends continue, humanity stands to lose a large portion of its natural inheritance. Extinction is one environmental problem that is truly irreversible—once gone, these species cannot be brought back.

What can be done? World Wildlife Fund (WWF), the global conservation organization,

China's giant panda clings to survival.

has been working since 1961 to conserve the diversity of life on earth. In recent years, WWF has advanced giant panda conservation by training more than 300 panda reserve staff and local government officials, working with the community to help save habitat and guard against illegal hunting. By spreading awareness of the danger of carbon dioxide emissions, and by promoting the use of renewable energy resources such as wind and solar power, WWF is trying to head off the effects of global warming, giving the polar bear a chance to survive. With the help of other organizations in Africa, WWF has established a system to monitor the status of mountain gorillas in order to be able to address potential threats.

The polar bear's habitat is at risk.

Why care about endangered animals? There are many reasons for protecting endangered species, including our own survival. Many of our foods and medicines come from wild species, and each wild species depends on a particular habitat for its food and shelter, and ultimately its survival. If one species in an ecosystem disappears, other species are affected. And when one ecosystem is altered or destroyed, a ripple effect occurs, and the interdependency of all living things becomes clear. Animals not only need protection to ensure their own species' survival, but they also serve as umbrella species; helping them helps numerous other species that live in the same habitat.

Beyond economics and human well-being, however, the rapid extinction of so many creatures on our planet raises profound ethical and moral questions. What sort of world will our children inherit? Do we want the future to be a place where pandas and gorillas only exist in captivity in zoos? If we are unable—or unwilling—to protect the animals we share our planet with, what does that say about humankind's future on earth?

For more information on WWF and its work, visit www.worldwildlife.org.

C **Understand from Context.** Use the context of the article to determine the meaning of the words and phrases.

1. **biodiversity** (line 1)
   a. endangered animals   **b.** the variety of living things   **c.** threats to nature

2. **habitat** (lines 4, 24, 28, and 61)
   a. the food animals eat   **b.** the place animals live   **c.** the extinction of animals

3. **extinction** (lines 12, 36, and 72)
   a. global warming   **b.** trying to protect animals   **c.** the disappearance of a species

4. **conservation** (lines 40 and 45)
   a. trying to protect animals   **b.** dangers to animals   **c.** feeding animals

5. **ecosystem** (lines 4, 63, and 64)
   a. trying to protect animals   **b.** threats to animals   **c.** how plants and animals work together

D **Critical Thinking.** Discuss the questions.

1. According to the article, what are some reasons animals become extinct? Can you think of any other reasons?

2. What arguments are given in the article to support animal conservation?

3. Look again at the last paragraph in the article. How would *you* answer the questions it raises?

NOW YOU CAN *Debate the value of animal conservation*

A **Frame Your Ideas.** Read and discuss the arguments for and against animal conservation. Which arguments are the strongest for each side of the animal conservation debate? Which are the weakest?

Pros	Cons
• Human beings have a responsibility to protect all living things.	• Extinctions are simply part of the natural process— it's the principle of "survival of the fittest."
• Species should be preserved for future generations.	• Environmental protection costs a lot of money. It's "a luxury" for countries that have more serious problems.
• Natural parks and wildlife are big tourist attractions— they generate jobs and income for local economies.	• Millions of species have already become extinct with no significant impact on the environment—it's no big deal.
• Species extinction at the current rate could lead to an ecological disaster.	• Conservation limits land available to farmers, who really need it for their livelihood.
• We miss the chance for new discoveries, such as medicines, with every species we lose.	• Do we really need 2,000 species of mice?
• Your own ideas:	• Your own ideas: ....

B **Debate.** Is it important to spend money on animal conservation? Form two groups— one for and one against. Take turns presenting your views.

C **Discussion.**

1. Why do you think some animals become endangered? What are some threats to the survival of animals in the wild?

2. In your opinion, are species worth saving even if they aren't "popular" or of any known value to people? Why or why not?

Writing: Express an opinion on animal treatment

Persuasion

To persuade readers to agree with your point of view, provide examples, facts, or experts' opinions that support your argument. Another effective technique is to demonstrate the weakness of opposing arguments. Summarize your main point in your concluding sentence.

Support your point of view	Offer experts' opinions
For example, . . .	[Smith] states that . . .
Another example is . . .	According to [Rivera], . . .
For instance, . . .	

Ways to discuss opposing arguments		Ways to conclude your argument
It can be argued that . . .		In conclusion, . . .
Some people think . . . } However,		In summary, . . .
It is true that . . .		To sum up, . . .

WRITING MODEL

Zoos play an important role in animal conservation. **For instance,** studies suggest that research is more easily conducted in zoos. **It can be argued that** animals should be free and that it is unethical to keep them in zoos. **However,** the survival of these species depends on scientific studies. **In conclusion,** animals should be kept in zoos in order to support conservation efforts.

A **Prewriting. Planning Your Argument.** Choose one of the questions in the following box or write your own question. State your opinion and list your arguments. Then think of possible opposing arguments.

- Is research on animals necessary in order to develop new medicines and procedures?
- Are some traditional forms of entertainment, such as circuses, bullfights, and cockfights, cruel to animals?
- Your own question: ....
....

Your opinion: ....

Your arguments:

1. ....

2. ....

3. ....

Possible opposing arguments:

1. ....

2. ....

3. ....

B **Writing.** On a separate sheet of paper, write a paragraph arguing your opinion from Prewriting. Remember to include a topic sentence at the beginning of the paragraph and a concluding sentence at the end.

C **Self-Check.**

☐ Did you state your point of view clearly?
☐ Did you provide examples, facts, or experts' opinions to support your point of view?
☐ Did you discuss opposing arguments?
☐ Did you include a topic sentence and a concluding sentence?

D **Peer Response.** Exchange paragraphs with a partner. Do you agree or disagree with your partner's point of view? Write a short response, explaining why. Start like this: I agree / disagree because . . . .

A 🎧 **Listening.** Listen to Part 1 of a radio program. Choose the phrase that best completes the statements, according to the listening.

1. Capuchin monkeys can be ....
   a. used for medical research **b.** loyal friends to humans **c.** trained to perform in circuses

2. These monkeys are useful to humans because they ....
   a. do simple jobs **b.** push a wheelchair **c.** wash dishes

B 🎧 Now listen to Part 2 and choose the phrase that best completes the statements.

1. Dolphin-assisted therapy had a positive effect on children's ....
   a. moral or ethical development **b.** speech development **c.** physical development

2. Children respond to dolphins because dolphins are ....
   a. good swimmers **b.** intelligent **c.** playful

3. Many of these children respond better to people after ....
   a. a year of treatment **b.** a few treatments **c.** a few weeks of treatment

C Change the adjective in each statement so it makes sense.

1. A relaxed pet that never bites is *destructive*. ....

2. A cat that bites or scratches people is *affectionate*. ....

3. A pet that likes to be with people is *aggressive*. ....

4. A dog that chews on shoes is *adorable*. ....

5. A pet that makes a mess is *sociable*. ....

D Complete each statement with an appropriate character trait.

1. A person who says or does unkind things to others is ....

2. People who can't pass a mirror without looking at themselves are ....

3. If one expresses oneself honestly to others, we say that person is ....

4. Someone who is too trusting of others is ....

5. People who think mainly about themselves are ....

6. People who are skillful at getting what they want are ....

7. If people have good judgment on matters of importance, we say they are ....

E Choose four of the topics from the box. Use modals with the passive voice to state your *own* opinion about each topic.

| endangered animals | hunting | pets |
| horseracing | bullfighting | zoos |

Example: *Hunting should be banned because it's inhumane.*

1. ....

2. ....

3. ....

4. ....

Advertising and Consumers

GOALS After Unit 7, you will be able to:

1 Give shopping advice
2 Discuss your reactions to ads
3 Persuade someone to buy a product
4 Describe consumer shopping habits

A **Topic Preview.** Look at the types of advertisements companies use to try to get consumers to buy products. What types of ads do you think you are most exposed to daily?

TV commercials

A BIKE THAT'S EASY TO CARE FOR. AND A BELT TO MATCH.

magazine ads

ads on trains, buses, or blimps

AQUAFINA GET SPOTTED

color perfectamen hermoso

Internet pop-ups

billboards

www.myweb.com.cn

Be the first to own one!

radio ads

B **Express Your Ideas.**

1. Which type of advertising do you find the most effective? Why?

2. Read the information to the right. Are you surprised by these statistics? Do you think they are similar for your country?

Daily Exposure to Advertising
In the United States, the average person is exposed to approximately 254 advertising messages each day—108 from TV, 34 from radio, and 112 from print. If you include brand labels on products and corporate logos on the sides of buildings, this number increases to over 1,000 ads per day.

Advertising Media Inter Center

C 🎧 3:02 **Sound Bites.** Read and listen to a couple talking about ads in a catalog.

BOB: I think it's about time I got myself one of these electric massage chairs.
ANN: What on earth for?
BOB: It would just be nice to have one. That's all.
ANN: Sounds like a waste of money to me. Don't they have anything useful in there?
BOB: See for yourself.
ANN: Now here's something I'd like to get my hands on—a self-watering flowerpot.
BOB: You've got to be kidding.
ANN: No, I'm not. I think one of these could come in really handy.

D **Focus on Language.** Read the conversation again. With a partner, find an expression in the conversation that is similar in meaning to each of the following statements or questions.

1. Why would you do that?
2. That's a useless thing to buy.
3. I'd really love to have one.
4. You can't be serious.
5. It might be very useful.

E **Relate to Personal Experience.** Tell your partner about something you'd really like to "get your hands on."

STARTING **POINT**

Discussion. What do you think of these products? Do you think any of them could be useful?

"I'd like to get my hands on one of these. It would really come in handy."

"You've got to be kidding. What a waste of money!"

Air Pollution Mask
Don't let polluted air ruin your health.

PORTA-BELLS
Wherever you are, just fill them with water and start your workout. Perfect for travel!

Riviera **Pool Chair**
Reclining seat and cup holders guarantee a great day at the pool.

4 Describe consumer shopping habits

A **Reading Warm-up.** Are you a careful shopper, or do you buy things on impulse?

B 🎧 3:12 **Reading.** Read the article. How is compulsive shopping a problem?

Compulsive Shopping: *The Real Cost*

Just in the last century, the way in which we consume material goods has shifted radically. For our grandparents, and some of our parents, shopping meant buying provisions to satisfy physical needs. Today, in addition to buying necessities, we shop to indulge ourselves in luxuries—high-priced gym shoes or the latest, most high-tech entertainment system. And we shop for the sheer fun of it. Most of us acquire continuously—everything from groceries to cars, from clothing to toiletries, from home furnishings to sporting equipment—and through our acquisitions, we express a sense of identity, taste, and lifestyle.

But some people go overboard. Their spending becomes excessive and often carries troubling consequences. Some people cannot resist the temptation, and very often they buy merely to acquire. This type of impulse buying can become so obsessive that people find themselves in considerable financial debt and psychological distress. Recent studies suggest that extreme impulse buying is on the increase, affecting an estimated 5 to 10 percent of the adult population in many countries.

We tend to define ourselves by what we buy and have. This often affects how we feel as well. For many, buying things on impulse is a way of avoiding or hiding feelings of anxiety and loneliness.

However, shopping as a way of dealing with internal distress is seldom effective for long. In fact, research suggests that people who consider shopping to be a priority in their lives tend to experience more anxiety and depression as well as a lower level of well-being than those who don't.

The long and short of it is this—you can't buy happiness.

Tips for Controlling Impulse Buying

- When you're just browsing and get the urge to buy something, ask yourself first if you really need it.
- Avoid sales. Spending any money on something you don't need is overspending.
- Follow the "24-hour rule." Don't buy anything new on the spot. Come back the next day if you think you really need it.
- Stick to a budget. Plan to splurge on the occasional wild purchase, but don't buy if it isn't in your budget.

On your ActiveBook disc: *Reading Glossary* and *Extra Reading Comprehension Questions*

Information source: www.theallengroup.com

C **Understand from Context.** Find these expressions in the article. Explain the meaning of each.

1. indulge ourselves
2. go overboard
3. resist the temptation
4. impulse buying
5. get the urge
6. overspending
7. splurge on

D **Relate to Personal Experience.** Discuss the questions.

1. According to the article, how have shopping habits changed over the last few generations? From your experience, do you agree?

2. Do you think compulsive shopping is a common problem? Do you know any compulsive shoppers? Give examples.

3. Do you think the tips in the article might be helpful for someone who wants to resist the temptation to overspend? Based on your experience, what tips would *you* suggest?

NOW YOU CAN   *Describe consumer shopping habits*

A **Frame Your Ideas.** Take the self-quiz. Check the statements that are true for you.

Are you a SHOPaholic?

☐ I sometimes feel guilty about how I spend my money shopping.

☐ When I'm feeling blue, it cheers me up to go shopping.

☐ When I go shopping, I can't resist the temptation to buy something—I just can't come home empty-handed.

☐ I feel uncomfortable if I haven't bought anything in a week.

☐ When I plan to go shopping for one item I need, I frequently end up coming home with a lot of things I *don't* need.

☐ I spend more than I have to in order to get more expensive designer names and labels.

☐ I can't pass up a good sale—even if I don't need anything, I just have to indulge myself.

☐ I sometimes lie to people about how much my purchases cost.

☐ I get more pleasure out of spending money than saving money.

☐ My shopping habits have caused problems in my personal relationships in some way.

Total the number of boxes you checked.

If your total is:

0-3 Great!
Keep up the good habits!

4-5 Not too bad!
Congratulations for admitting you're not perfect!

6-8 Uh-oh!
Sounds like trouble may be around the corner! It's time to tighten your purse strings.

9-10 Red alert!
It's time to take the bull by the horns and change some of the ways you shop and spend money.

B **Discussion.** Choose one of the following topics and meet in small groups with other classmates who have chosen the same one. Share your conclusions with the class.

1. Do you think most people tend to go overboard with their shopping? Explain.
2. Do you think people are too influenced by advertising? Explain.
3. Should people only spend money on things they need and never on things they don't need? Is it OK to buy on impulse sometimes? Is it OK to splurge once in a while?

C **Project.** Create a class newsletter with articles about consumer shopping habits and responsible shopping.

Writing: *Explain an article you read*

Summarize and Paraphrase Another Person's Ideas

A summary is a shortened explanation of the main ideas of an article. When writing a summary, include only the author's main points, not your own reactions or opinions. Be sure to paraphrase what the author says, instead of just copying the author's exact words.

To summarize an article, focus on main ideas and the most important supporting details. Use the following reporting verbs to paraphrase the writer's ideas: <u>state</u>, <u>argue</u>, <u>report</u>, <u>believe</u>, <u>explain</u>, <u>point out</u>, and <u>conclude</u>.

The article **states** that . . .   The journalist **reports** that . . .

The writer **points out** that . . .   The author **concludes** that . . .

Some other common expressions for reporting another person's ideas:

According to [Smith], . . .   **As** [the article] explains, . . .

In [the writer's] **opinion**, . . .   **From** [García's] **point of view**, . . .

PARAPHRASING

When you paraphrase what a person says, you say it in your *own* words.

The author: "But some people go overboard. Their spending becomes excessive and often carries troubling consequences. Some people cannot resist the temptation, and very often they buy merely to acquire."

You: *The author points out that it is difficult for some people not to buy things on impulse. They just buy anything they want.*

A **Prewriting. Identifying Main Ideas.** Read the article "Compulsive Shopping: The Real Cost" on page 82 and underline the important parts. Then read the article again and identify the main ideas below.

Main idea of paragraph 1:
Main idea of paragraph 2:
Main idea of paragraph 3:
Main idea of paragraph 4:

B **Writing.** On a separate sheet of paper, combine the main ideas to write your summary. Be sure to paraphrase what the author says, using your *own* words. Your summary should be no more than four to six sentences long.

C **Self-Check.**

☐ Is your summary a lot shorter than the original article?

☐ Does your summary include only the author's main ideas?

☐ Did you paraphrase the author's ideas?

☐ Did you include your opinion of the article? If so, rewrite the summary without it.

Review

A 🎧 **Listening.** Listen to the conversations about prices. Then read the statements and listen again. Circle the phrase that best completes each statement, according to what the people say.

1. **a.** The woman thinks the price of the first vase is (a bit steep / a real bargain). The man thinks it's (a steal / a rip-off).
   b. The woman thinks the second vase is (a steal / a good deal). The man thinks it's (a rip-off / no bargain).

2. **a.** The woman thinks the exercise bike from Freeman's was (a great offer / a rip-off). The man thinks it was (no bargain / a steal).
   b. The woman thinks the price of the bike from Mason's is (a bit steep / a great deal). The man thinks it's (a better offer / no deal).

3. **a.** The man thinks the price of the necklace is (a bit steep / no deal). The woman thinks it's (pretty steep / a bargain).
   b. The man thinks the earrings are (a good deal / a rip-off). The woman thinks they're (a great deal / no bargain).

B Complete each statement with your *own* ideas.

Example: *Watching old Charlie Chaplin movies always* cracks me up.

1. .... cracks me up.
2. .... blows me away.
3. .... chokes me up.
4. .... gets on my nerves.

C Complete the statements with passive forms of gerunds or infinitives. Use <u>being</u> or <u>to be</u>.

1. I don't recall .... any information.
   (send)
2. They want .... more time for the project.
   (give)
3. She arranged .... to the airport.
   (take)
4. I was disappointed .... the news.
   (tell)
5. He risked .... from his job.
   (fire)
6. We were delighted .... to the wedding.
   (invite)

D On a separate sheet of paper, answer the questions in your *own* way.

1. What kinds of things do you like to splurge on?
2. Have you ever gone a little overboard buying something? Explain.
3. What can't you resist the temptation to do? Why?

Family Trends

GOALS After Unit 8, you will be able to:

1 Describe family trends
2 Discuss parent / teen issues
3 Compare generations
4 Describe care for the elderly

A **Topic Preview.** Look at the two cartoons about families. Then answer the questions with a partner.

"Because this family isn't ready to hold democratic elections—that's why!"

1. Who do you think was speaking before the father spoke? What do you think was said?

2. Is your family a "democracy"? How do decisions get made?

3. What didn't the father have when he was young that the son has now? Do you think the father has a good point, or is he being ridiculous?

4. In your family, is there a "generation gap" between older and younger family members? Explain.

"You have it easy. When I was your age, I had to walk all the way across the room to change the channel."

B **Express Your Ideas.** Do you think the cartoons are funny? Do you think they portray typical families? Why or why not?

C 3:14 🎧 **Sound Bites.** Read and listen to a conversation about relationships.

Sam

Margaret

TERESA: Did you hear that Sam and Margaret got back together?
BETTINA: Wow! I didn't even know they'd split up! It shows you how out of touch I am.
TERESA: Well, they had this major falling out about two months ago, and they separated. But it looks like they've patched things up.
BETTINA: Good. They're a nice couple. I hope things work out for them.
TERESA: Me too. So, how's *your* family?
BETTINA: Not bad, but we've been having some trouble with our son.
TERESA: Really? What kind of trouble?
BETTINA: Well, he's been acting up in school. You know, talking back to his teachers, not doing his homework.
TERESA: Eric? I can't believe it! He's always been so well-behaved!
BETTINA: Well, I told him he's grounded until he shapes up. No movies, no games, no trips to the mall.
TERESA: Smart move. Eric's a good kid, but you don't want him to turn into a troublemaker.

D **Paraphrase.** With a partner, use the context of the conversation to restate each of the following sentences in your own words.

1. They **got back together**.
2. They **split up**.
3. They **had a falling out**.
4. They **patched things up**.
5. Things **didn't work out**.

6. My kids have been **acting up**.
7. Don't **talk back**!
8. Your son is so **well-behaved**.
9. He'd better **shape up**!
10. That kid is such **a troublemaker**.

E **Express and Support an Opinion.** Do you think grounding Eric is a smart move? In your opinion, what's the best way to handle or discipline a teenager who has been acting up?

STARTING **POINT**

Relate to Personal Experience. Choose one of the topics. Tell your partner about a time you …

had a difference of opinion with someone from another generation.

helped patch things up for someone else.

had a falling out with a friend, a family member, or a colleague.

A 🎧 3:15 **Grammar Snapshot.** Read the information in the brochure and notice the comparatives.

Falling Birthrates

Current trends show the size of families is changing, impacting societies worldwide. Women are marrying later, and couples are waiting longer to have children. And **the longer** couples wait to have children, **the fewer** children they have.

Two key factors that impact family size are the education and the employment of women. Studies show that **the more** education women get, **the smaller** families they have. Moreover, **the longer** women stay in school, **the better** their opportunities for employment. Working women are less likely to marry young and have large families.

In addition to the falling birthrate, there is a rising life expectancy. With people living **longer and longer**, families are going to have to face the challenges posed by an aging population. **The longer** people live, **the more** care they require. Traditionally, children have cared for their elderly parents at home. However, **the more** the birthrate falls, **the harder** the future may be for the elderly. With fewer children, families may find it **more and more** difficult to care for their older members.

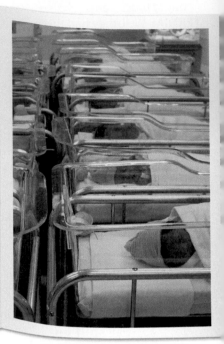

Information source: United Nations Statistics Division

B **Identify Cause and Effect.** Discuss the questions.

1. According to the brochure, what factors explain why more couples are having fewer children?

2. Why do you think populations are living longer? What problems does a larger elderly population pose?

C **Grammar.** Repeated comparatives and double comparatives

Repeated comparatives are used to describe actions and things that are increasing or decreasing.
The birthrate is getting **lower and lower**.
By the end of the twentieth century, couples were waiting **longer and longer** to marry.
More and more people are marrying later.
Fewer and fewer children are leaving school.
It's becoming **more and more** difficult.

Double comparatives are used to describe a cause-and-effect process.
The more education women get, **the later** they marry. [Women are getting more education, so they're marrying later.]
The less children studied, **the more slowly** they learned. [Children studied less, so they learned more slowly.]

NOTE: When <u>be</u> is used in double comparatives, it is sometimes omitted.
The better the quality of health care (is), **the higher** the life expectancy (is).

BE CAREFUL! Don't use continuous verb forms in double comparatives.
The longer couples **wait** to have children, the fewer children they **have**.
NOT The longer couples ~~are waiting~~ to have children, the fewer they~~'re having~~.

> **GRAMMAR BOOSTER** ▸ p. G13
> • Making comparisons: summary
> • Other uses of comparatives, superlatives, and comparisons with <u>as</u> … <u>as</u>

D **Grammar Practice.** Complete each statement logically, using double comparatives.

1. .... people are when they marry, ... children they have.
   (old)   (few)

2. .... the life expectancy, ... the elderly population is.
   (high)   (large)

3. .... people work, ... they are.
   (hard)   (successful)

4. .... the quality of health care is, ... the death rate.
   (good)   (low)

5. .... the country is, ... the life expectancy.
   (developed)   (low)

6. .... women are when they have children, ... they are to get a higher education.
   (young)   (likely)

E 🎧 **Listening. Listen to Apply Grammar.** Listen to three people talking about trends in marriage and family life. Then listen again and complete each statement, according to what the speaker implies, using double comparatives.

1. .... education mothers get, ... medical care they receive.

2. .... couples date, ... they marry.

3. .... children stay in school, ... their life expectancy.

NOW YOU CAN   *Describe family trends*

A **Frame Your Ideas.** With a partner, use repeated comparatives to write examples of the ways families are changing in your country.

> *"People are getting married **later and later**."*

IDEAS
- birthrate
- life expectancy
- age at marriage
- health
- education
- income
- employment opportunities
- generational differences

B **Summarize.** On a separate sheet of paper, summarize the changes you've discussed. Use repeated comparatives and double comparatives.

> *In the last few decades, family size has declined. Fewer and fewer people are having big families, so their standard of living is higher. The higher the standard of living is, the healthier the population.*

C **Use the Grammar.** In small groups, compare the trends you've identified. How will these changes impact families in the future?

> *"It seems like **more and more** people are having fewer children. This could be a problem later because...."*

2 GOAL
Discuss parent / teen issues

A 🎧 3:17 **Conversation Snapshot.** Read and listen.
Notice the conversation strategies.

A: What do you think parents should do if their
teenage kids start smoking?

B: Well, **I hate to say it, but** there's not much they can do.

A: Why's that?

B: Well, teenagers are out of the house most of the day,
so parents can't control everything they do.

A: **I suppose. But** they can ground them if they
don't shape up.

🎧 3:18 **Rhythm and intonation practice**

🎧 3:19 **Examples of bad behavior**
- acting up at school
- staying out late without permission
- being rude and disrespectful
- becoming a troublemaker

B 🎧 3:20 **Vocabulary. Describing Parent and Teen Behavior.** Listen and practice.

Parents can sometimes be . . .

(too) strict

They set a lot of restrictions and
expect kids to obey rules.

(too) lenient

They let their kids have or do anything
they want.

overprotective

They worry too much about their kids.

Teenagers can sometimes be . . .

rebellious

They refuse to follow rules and do the
opposite of what is expected of them.

spoiled

They expect to have or do whatever
they want.

disrespectful

They are rude to adults and think what
adults say is not important.

C **Vocabulary Practice.** Correct the adjective in each of the following statements.

1. Parents who always allow their teenage children to stay out late are *overprotective*.

2. Teenagers who demand that their parents buy everything they ask for are *rebellious*.

3. When parents never let their children do things because they are afraid that their children
will get sick or hurt, they are being *strict*.

4. When a teen gets a tattoo against a parent's wishes, we say that he or she is *disrespectful*.

5. Parents who make their teenage children clean their rooms every day are *lenient*.

6. Teens who don't listen to adults and often talk back are *spoiled*.

D 🎧 3:21 **Listening. Listen to Activate Vocabulary.** Listen to the conversations about parent and teen behavior. Then listen again and determine which adjective from the Vocabulary best completes each statement.

1. She thinks he's _____.

2. She thinks he's acting _____.

3. He thinks she's _____.

4. He's angry because she's being _____.

5. He thinks she's _____.

6. She criticizes him for being _____.

E **Make Personal Comparisons.** Can you identify with any of the people in the listening? Are any of the speakers like anyone you know? Explain.

NOW YOU CAN   *Discuss parent / teen issues*

A **Frame Your Ideas.** Discuss and complete the survey with a partner. Compare your ideas. Give specific examples to support your answers.

Circle the rating that most closely expresses your opinion.

1 = completely agree   **2** = somewhat agree, depending on the circumstances   **3** = completely disagree

PARENTS		Me	My partner
	Parents should let kids make their own mistakes. Being overprotective with children makes kids less responsible.	1 2 3	1 2 3
	It's OK to give in to kids' demands sometimes in order to "keep the peace."	1 2 3	1 2 3
	Parents should include their children in family decision-making. After all, kids' opinions are important, too.	1 2 3	1 2 3
	It's a good idea for parents to use physical punishment to discipline their children. If parents aren't strict, their kids will become troublemakers.	1 2 3	1 2 3
	Your own idea:		1 2 3

TEENS		Me	My partner
	Teenagers don't always have to obey their parents. Sometimes it's OK to say "no."	1 2 3	1 2 3
	Teenagers shouldn't have to help around the house. They already have enough to do with their schoolwork.	1 2 3	1 2 3
	Teenagers are mature enough to make their own decisions. They shouldn't have to ask permission for everything.	1 2 3	1 2 3
	Teenagers have a right to privacy. They shouldn't have to tell their parents about everything they do.	1 2 3	1 2 3
	Your own idea:		1 2 3

B **Use the Conversation Strategies.** Role-play a conversation in which you discuss parent or teen behavior. Use the Conversation Snapshot as a guide. Start like this:

"What do you think parents should do if their teenage kids ...?"   OR   "What do you think kids should do if their parents ...?"

C **Discussion.** If you could give parents one piece of advice, what would it be? If you could give teenagers one piece of advice, what would it be?

3 GOAL
Compare generations

A 🎧 3:22 **Word Skills. Transforming Verbs and Adjectives into Nouns**

common noun endings	nouns		common noun endings	nouns	
-ation -tion -ssion	expect → explain → frustrate → permit →	**expectation** **explanation** **frustration** **permission**	-ness	fair → rebellious → selfish → strict →	**fairness** **rebelliousness** **selfishness** **strictness**
-ment	develop → involve →	**development** **involvement**	-ity	generous → mature → mobile → secure →	**generosity** **maturity** **mobility** **security**
-y	courteous → difficult →	**courtesy** **difficulty**			
-ility	responsible → reliable → capable → dependable →	**responsibility** **reliability** **capability** **dependability**	-ance -ence	important → independent → lenient → obedient →	**importance** **independence** **lenience** **obedience**

NOTE: Sometimes internal spelling changes occur when a noun ending is added to a verb or an adjective.

> **PRONUNCIATION BOOSTER** ▸ p. P7
> • Stress placement

B **Word Skills Practice.** Circle all the words that are nouns. Check in a dictionary if you are not sure about the meaning of a word.

1. dependency   depend   dependence   dependent
2. impatient   impatience   impatiently
3. confidence   confident   confide   confidently
4. unfair   unfairness   unfairly
5. consider   consideration   considerate   considerately
6. closeness   close   closely
7. different   difference   differentiate   differentiation
8. happily   happy   happiness
9. attraction   attract   attractive   attractiveness

Vilnius, the capital of Lithuania

C 🎧 3:23 **Listening. Listen to Summarize.** Listen to Part 1 of a man's description of the generation gap in his family. Then answer the questions.

1. How did Rimas grow up differently from his parents?
2. Why does Rimas's father think teenagers nowadays have more problems than when he was growing up?

D 🎧 3:24 **Listening. Listen for Details.** Listen to Part 1 again. Then complete each statement.

1. Rimas grew up in _____, but his parents grew up in _____.
2. Rimas's extended family includes _____ aunts and uncles on his mother's side.
3. When Rimas's mother was growing up, every evening she ate dinner _____. However, when Rimas and his sister were kids, they sometimes had to eat _____.

Rimas Vilkas

E 3:25 🎧 **Listening. Compare and Contrast.** Now listen to Part 2. Then listen again and complete the chart by describing the differences between the two generations. Compare your chart with a partner's.

	How are they different?	
	Rimas's parents' generation	Rimas's generation
career choices		
mobility		
influences from other cultures		
age at marriage and childbearing		
work experience		
closeness of family		

F **Critical Thinking.** Discuss the questions.

1. Why do Rimas's parents worry about him and the future? Why do you think parents always worry about their children?

2. In what ways is the Vilkas's family story similar to or different from yours?

NOW YOU CAN *Compare generations*

A **Notepadding.** Compare your parents' generation with your generation. Write your ideas on your notepad. Discuss them with a partner.

	My parents' generation	My generation
music		
style of clothes		
hairstyles / facial hair		
attitude toward elders		
family responsibility		
language (idioms, slang)		
marriage and childbearing		
values and beliefs		
other:		

B **Discussion.**

1. In what ways is your generation most different from your parents' generation? What do you like best or respect most about your parents' generation?

2. What contributions do you think your generation will make to the next generation? How do you think the next generation will differ from yours?

Describe care for the elderly

A **Reading Warm-up.** In previous generations, how have older family members traditionally been cared for in your country?

B 🎧 3:26 **Reading.** Read the article. What impact has China's one-child policy had on care for the elderly?

Uncertain Future for China's Elderly

Due to a sharp increase in its aging population, China faces new social problems in the future, according to a recent report from the Chinese Academy of Sciences. In China today, the elderly—people aged 60 or older—make up about 11 percent of the population. However, according to United Nations statistics, by 2050 the number of elderly will increase to more than 31 percent. If this trend continues, the elderly could eventually outnumber young people—a dramatic change for China.

While lower birthrates and higher life expectancies are causing similar population shifts in many countries, this transformation is happening faster in China due to the strict one-child policy introduced in 1979. Under this policy, couples can have only one child. The policy's purpose was to stop China's burgeoning population from growing too fast. It created a generation of "only children" growing up without brothers or sisters who can share the burden of caring for elderly family members.

According to Chinese tradition, the elderly have always been honored and respected by the young; for generations, parents and grandparents have relied on their children to care for them in old age. But today an increasing number of single young adults face the

difficult situation of caring for both their parents and their grandparents. This phenomenon is known as a 4-2-1 family: For every *one* child, there are *two* parents and *four* grandparents to look after. Breaking with tradition, many young adults who can afford it are beginning to transfer the responsibility of looking after their elderly relatives to private nursing homes. This change in attitude is causing some conflict and anger between generations.

The aging of China's population will have a big impact on the country's future. The less the old can depend on the young, the more they may have to depend on the government. In one attempt to deal with this problem, the government has started a national lottery to raise money for elder care. However, it may still need to create more resources to care for its graying population.

China's one-child families have had an unexpected effect on care for the elderly.

On your ActiveBook disc: *Reading Glossary* and *Extra Reading Comprehension Questions*

Information source: *Beijing Times*

C **Summarize.** Describe how China's population is changing. What is causing those changes?

D **Confirm Content.** Discuss the questions.

1. According to the article, what challenges are China's young people facing today?
2. How may elder care in China differ in the future from the traditions of the past?

A **Frame Your Ideas.** With a partner, discuss the statements and check those you think are true about care for the elderly in your country.

- ☐ Most elderly people are adequately cared for.
- ☐ The way the elderly are cared for has been changing.
- ☐ The elderly usually live with younger family members.
- ☐ The elderly usually live in their own homes or apartments.
- ☐ The elderly usually live in special nursing homes.
- ☐ The government makes sure the elderly have affordable care.
- ☐ Younger people accept care for elderly relatives as their responsibility.
- ☐ Older people generally prefer not to socialize with younger people.
- ☐ Other: ....

B **Draw Conclusions.** Read each case study. Discuss the challenges each person is facing and recommend solutions.

Ingrid is divorced and has three young daughters. Her mother died years ago, and her seventy-five-year-old father can no longer take care of himself. He often forgets things. She worries that he might get hurt.

Robert's parents, who live in another city, are in their eighties. They continue to have a full social life, and they still enjoy traveling with organized tours. But they are not as strong as they used to be and need help with cooking and cleaning.

Nick is married and has two teenage children. His mother just turned seventy-nine and lives alone. Nick and his family live in a very small apartment with two bedrooms. He and his wife both work overtime, putting in long hours in order to make ends meet. Nick is concerned about his mother's health and well-being.

C **Discussion.** How do you think the elderly will be cared for by the time you are old? How would *you* like to be cared for? Describe the ideal situation for elder care. Use language from the checklist in A. Frame Your Ideas.

D **Project.** Prepare a presentation about how the elderly are cared for in your country.

Writing: *Describe your relationship with a family member*

Avoiding Run-on Sentences and Comma Splices

Note two common errors that writers often make when joining two sentences.

Run-on sentence (connecting sentences without using punctuation)
INCORRECT: My grandmother taught me how to bake however I never do.

Comma splice (connecting two sentences with a comma and no conjunction)
INCORRECT: My grandmother taught me how to bake, now I know how to make great cookies.

To correct a run-on sentence or a comma splice, choose one of the following:

- Use a period and capitalize the following word.

  My grandmother taught me how to bake. Now I know how to make great cookies.
  My grandmother taught me how to bake. However, I never do.

- Use a semicolon.

  My grandmother taught me how to bake; now I know how to make great cookies.
  My grandmother taught me how to bake; however, I never do.

- Use a comma and a coordinating conjunction.

  My grandmother taught me how to bake, and now I know how to make great cookies.
  My grandmother taught me how to bake, but I never do.

Coordinating conjunctions

and	for	or	yet
but	nor	so	

ERROR CORRECTION | Correct the errors.

Everyone tells me I am a great cook however, everything I know about baking I learned from my grandmother. I always helped my grandmother when she baked we made cookies, cakes, pies, and breads together. I even had more fun baking than eating the food! At first I wondered how she was able to put various ingredients together without measuring cups and written recipes with time, I also learned the tricks. When my grandmother died, she left me all her baking and cooking equipment and many years of wonderful memories.

A **Prewriting. "Freewriting" to Generate Ideas.**
Writing quickly without stopping is one way to generate ideas. First, choose a family relationship you would like to write about. Then, write anything that comes to mind for five minutes. Write quickly and do not worry about spelling, punctuation, etc. Finally, read what you wrote. Select some of the ideas from your freewriting and organize them logically.

My grandparents
—in their seventies
—always help me
—grandfather likes to fish
—grandmother loves when I visit

B **Writing.** On a separate sheet of paper, write a paragraph about the relationship you chose. Include a topic sentence that expresses your main idea. Avoid run-on sentences and comma splices.

C **Self-Check.**

☐ Did you write any run-on sentences? Comma splices? If so, correct them.
☐ Do all the sentences support the topic sentence?
☐ Is the paragraph interesting? What could you add to make it more interesting?

ActiveBook: *More Practice*

grammar · vocabulary · listening
reading · speaking · pronunciation

A 🎧 **Listening.** Listen to the conversations about generational issues. Then listen to each conversation again and complete each statement with the correct comparative.

1. Philip is spending .... time on his homework.
   a. more and more   **b.** less and less

2. .... , the more her mother worries.
   a. The later Sandi stays out   **b.** The older Sandi gets

3. The stricter Jill's father gets, ... she becomes.
   a. the more rebellious   **b.** the more spoiled

4. The older the sisters get, ...
   a. the smarter they become   **b.** the more they appreciate their parents

B Write the adjective that best describes the behavior in each statement.

1. Mark's parents don't allow him to watch more than two hours of TV a day, but most of his friends can watch as much as they want. He feels that his parents are ....

2. Karen has a closet full of expensive clothes, yet she always complains about not having anything to wear. Her parents usually buy her whatever she wants. A lot of people think Karen is ....

3. Even though she has had her driver's license for a year and a half, Marissa's parents worry about her driving at night. They say that it's too dangerous, but Marissa thinks they're just being ....

4. When Clyde's grandfather asked him to turn down the volume on his CD player, he ignored him and continued to listen to his music. Clyde's grandfather thought this was very ....

5. Rodney and Carolyn believe parents don't need to be so concerned about their children. They rarely set rules for their kids. Carolyn's sister thinks this is a bad idea. She feels they're ....

6. Deanna wears clothing that her parents find shocking. She also has friends that her parents don't approve of. Her mother wishes she weren't so ....

C Correct the part of speech of any of the incorrect underlined words.

1. Teenagers were given a lot more <u>responsibility</u> when I was young.

2. I think teenagers today lack the <u>mature</u> to make decisions for themselves.

3. The main reason young people are rebellious today is <u>selfishness</u>.

4. If kids today were taught about <u>courteous</u>, they would be better behaved.

5. There's no question that teenagers today demand more <u>independent</u> than they did fifty years ago.

6. It's important to be involved in your child's <u>development</u>.

7. Young people have a lot more <u>mobile</u> than they did several generations ago.

8. It seems like there's a lot more <u>rebellious</u> among teenagers today.

History's Mysteries

GOALS
1 Speculate about the out-of-the-ordin
2 Present a theory about a past event
3 Discuss how believable a story is
4 Evaluate the trustworthiness of news sources

A **Topic Preview.** Take the quiz with a partner and discuss your answers.

The World's Easiest Quiz . . .

or is it?

How long did the Hundred Years' War last? The answer *has* to be a hundred years, right? Well, the answer may not be what you think. Take a stab at this quiz and see how many answers you can guess correctly. Then check your answers below.

1. How long did the Hundred Years' War in Western Europe last?
a. 100 years   c. 50 years
b. 116 years   d. 200 years

2. Which country makes Panama hats?
a. Panama
b. the Philippines
c. Ecuador
d. Italy

3. From which animals do we get catgut for violin strings?
a. cats   c. sharks
b. sheep   d. dogs

4. The former U.S.S.R. used to celebrate the October Revolution in which month?
a. October   c. December
b. November   d. June

5. What is a camel hair paintbrush made of?
a. camel hair   c. cat hair
b. squirrel hair   d. human hair

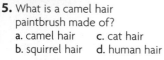

6. The Canary Islands in the Atlantic Ocean are named after what animal?
a. the canary   c. the dog
b. the cat   d. the camel

7. What was King George VI of England's first name?
a. George   c. Jose
b. Charles   d. Albert

8. What color is a male purple finch?
a. dark purple   c. sky blue
b. crimson red   d. white

9. What country do Chinese gooseberries come from?
a. China   c. Sweden
b. Japan   d. New Zealand

10. How long did the Thirty Years' War in Central Europe last?
a. 30 years   c. 20 years
b. 40 years   d. 100 years

SCORING	
1–2 correct	Hmm . . . Maybe you need to work on your guessing skills!
3–5 correct	Not a bad job at guessing! Or did you already know a few of the answers?
6–10 correct	Either you're a great guesser, or you're a real scholar!

ANSWERS: 1. b. 116 years (The war ran from 1337 to 1453, but with interruptions.) **2. c.** Ecuador (In the 16th century, the hats were shipped through the Panama Canal.) **3. b.** sheep (Catgut comes from the German *kitgut*, a type of violin.) **4. b.** November (Russians used to use the Julian calendar, which was different from the Gregorian calendar by 13 days.) **5. b.** squirrel hair (The brush was named after its inventor, whose surname was Camel.) **6. c.** the dog (The word *canary* comes from the Latin *Insularia Canaria*—Island of the Dogs.) **7. d.** Albert (British kings usually take new names.) **8. b.** crimson red (This is the only "red finch" with purple on its chest.) **9. d.** New Zealand (New Zealanders renamed them kiwi fruit to avoid confusion.) **10. a.** 30 years, of course! (The war lasted from 1618 to 1648.)

B **Express Your Ideas.** Did you have a reason for the answers you chose? Did you just take "wild guesses," or did you use "the process of elimination"? Which method do you think works better? Why?

C 🎧 4:02 **Sound Bites.** Read and listen to a conversation about a well-known mystery.

VICTOR: I saw the most fascinating TV program about Bigfoot last night.
PATTY: Bigfoot? Don't tell me you buy that story!
VICTOR: You're such a skeptic! Who's to say those things don't exist? How else would you explain all those sightings over the years?
PATTY: Could've been gorillas.
VICTOR: In the U.S.? I don't think so. There's no question—Bigfoot is real.
PATTY: Get out of here! There's no such thing as Bigfoot. You have such a wild imagination!
VICTOR: You'd change your mind if you'd seen that program.
PATTY: The only way I'd change my mind is if I saw one of them with my own two eyes. Seeing is believing, as far as I'm concerned.

Bigfoot

Many people claim to have seen a hairy, human-like creature—called "Bigfoot"—in the western mountains of the United States. In 2004, Bob Heironimus admitted that he dressed in a costume for this famous 1967 image.

D **Think and Explain.** Read the conversation again. With a partner, explain the meaning of each of the following statements.

1. "Don't tell me you buy that story!"

2. "You're such a skeptic!"

3. "There's no question—Bigfoot is real."

4. "Get out of here!"

5. "You have such a wild imagination!"

6. "Seeing is believing."

E **Activate Prior Knowledge.** With a partner, discuss other mysteries you've heard about.

STARTING **POINT**

Draw Conclusions. Read about these two mysteries. How possible is it that each is true? Discuss your opinions with a partner. Use the expressions from Exercise D.

The Loch Ness Monster

For centuries, people have reported sightings of a very large, unfamiliar animal living in the deepest lake in the United Kingdom — Scotland's Loch Ness.

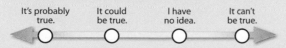

It's probably true.   It could be true.   I have no idea.   It can't be true.

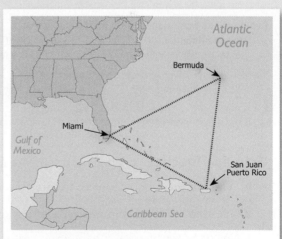

The Bermuda Triangle

Over several centuries, in a triangular area of the Caribbean Sea, numerous ships have mysteriously disappeared—never to be seen again. Many believe that there is something about that area that causes ships simply to disappear into thin air.

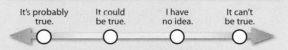

It's probably true.   It could be true.   I have no idea.   It can't be true.

GOAL
Speculate about the out-of-the-ordinary

A 🎧 **Conversation Snapshot.** Read and listen. Notice the conversation strategies.

A: I wonder where Stacey is.
She said she'd be here by ten.

B: Do you think something happened?

A: Beats me.

B: Well, I'm sure it's nothing.
I'll bet she's stuck in traffic.

A: You're probably right.

B: Why else would she be late?

A: I can't imagine.

🎧 **Rhythm and intonation practice**

> 4:05
> 🎧 **Ways to say "I don't know."**
>
> Beats me.
> I can't imagine.
> I don't have a clue.
> I have no idea.
> Your guess is as good as mine.
> You got me.
> Who knows?

B **Grammar.** Indirect speech with modals

> **GRAMMAR BOOSTER**
> ▸ p. G14
> • Say, ask, and tell: summary
> • Other reporting verbs

REMEMBER: When a reporting verb is in a past form, the verb in the indirect speech statement usually changes or "backshifts."

"I **went** to the store." → She said [that] she **had gone** to the store.

Some modals also backshift in indirect speech.

"I'll be there by six." → I said [that] I **would** be there by six.
"You **must** come on time." → She said [that] they **had to** come on time.
"You **have to*** pay in cash." → They told me [that] I **had to** pay in cash.

Some modals don't backshift in indirect speech.

"You **should** hurry." → She told him [that] he **should** hurry.
"He **might** call tonight." → He said [that] he **might** call tonight.

Perfect modals never backshift in indirect speech.

"We **must have** forgotten." → He said [that] they **must have** forgotten.

Modals that backshift	Modals that don't backshift
will → would	would → would
can → could	could → could
may → might	might → might
must → had to	should → should
have to → had to	ought to → ought to

> **REMEMBER**
>
> In indirect speech, pronouns and possessives change in order to preserve the speaker's meaning.
> "**My** brother got **me** a gift." → She said [that] **her** brother had gotten **her** a gift.

** Have to is not a true modal, but it is often referred to as a "modal-like expression."

C **Grammar Practice.** Change each sentence from direct to indirect speech.

1. He told me, "You shouldn't worry if I arrive a little late." ....

2. He said, "Students must arrive fifteen minutes early." ....

3. "Jack may have gotten lost," he said. ....

4. "They might have forgotten their luggage," she said. ....

5. She told me, "I'll call you as soon as I get there." ....

6. She told us, "I may have to cancel the meeting." ....

7. He told me, "I'll come early." ....

8. "You ought to phone first," she told me. ....

D 🎧 **Vocabulary. Ways to Express Certainty.** Listen and practice.

very certain	
Clearly It's obvious } he's not coming. There's no question	

almost certain	
Most likely Probably } someone found it. I'll bet	

somewhat certain	
I guess I imagine } she's lost. I suppose	

not certain	
Maybe It's possible } he forgot. It could be	

NOW YOU CAN *Speculate about the out-of-the-ordinary*

A **Use the Vocabulary.** With a partner, discuss and speculate about one of the situations below, or create your own. Then on a separate sheet of paper, use the Vocabulary to write four sentences about the situation in which you are very certain, almost certain, somewhat certain, and not certain.

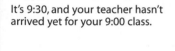
I'll bet the elevator isn't working.

You're trying to take the elevator downstairs to get some lunch. You've been waiting for the elevator for over ten minutes.

It's 9:30, and your teacher hasn't arrived yet for your 9:00 class.

CLASS BEGINS 9:00

You expected a package to arrive on Monday. It's Friday, and it still hasn't come.

B **Use the Conversation Strategies.** Role-play the situation you chose, or choose another one, speculating about what you think happened. Use the Vocabulary and the Conversation Snapshot as a guide. Start like this: "I wonder..."

You go to your favorite restaurant. The lights are on, but the doors are locked, and there's no one inside.

101

2 GOAL
Present a theory about a past event

A 🎧 4:07 **Grammar Snapshot.** Read the articles and notice the perfect modals in the passive voice.

THE STONE BALLS OF COSTA RICA

One of the strangest mysteries in archaeology was discovered in the Diquis Delta of Costa Rica. Since the 1930s, hundreds of stone balls have been found, ranging in size from a few centimeters to over two meters in diameter. Some weigh as much as 16 tons. Almost all of them are made of hard stone and are clearly made by human hands. Nobody knows for sure, but it's believed that the balls **could have been made** by the ancestors of native peoples who lived in the region at the time of the Spanish conquest. But what they **might have been used** for is a total mystery.

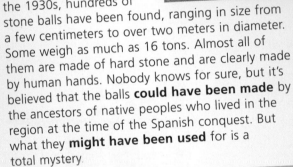

Information source: www.world-mysteries.com

An Explosion in Tunguska

At 7:17 A.M. on June 30, 1908, an explosion of catastrophic proportions occurred in the forests of Tunguska in northern Siberia, 3,540 kilometers east of Moscow. All over Europe there were reports of strange colors in the sky. It was impossible to investigate the incident because it was so far from where people lived at the time. Most scientists assume that the area **must have been struck** by a huge meteorite. But there are some researchers who claim that the area **couldn't have been hit** by a meteorite because there was no evidence of a crater—the type of hole a meteorite would have caused.

Information source: en.wikipedia.org

B **Activate Prior Knowledge.** Are you familiar with either of these stories? Have you heard about any other similar mysteries? Describe them.

C **Grammar. Perfect modals in the passive voice for speculating about the past**

You can use <u>may</u>, <u>might</u>, <u>could</u>, <u>must</u>, or <u>had to</u> to speculate with different degrees of certainty about the past. Use the passive voice if the performer of the action is unknown or if you want to focus on the receiver of the action.

not certain
- The dinosaurs **might (or may) have been killed** by a meteor.
- The trees **could have been destroyed** by a fire.
- The gold figures **might not (or may not) have been lost**.

almost certain
- The stone balls **must have been moved** using animals.
- The drawings **must not have been discovered** until later.

very certain
- The crater **had to have been caused** by a meteorite.
- The trees **couldn't (or can't) have been burned** in a fire.

Short responses with perfect modals in the passive voice

Is it possible they were killed by a meteorite?	They **may have been**.
Do you think they were made by hand?	They **had to have been**.
I wonder if they could have just been lost.	They **couldn't have been**.
Could they have been stolen?	They **might have been**.

D **Grammar Practice.** Complete each conversation about these sensational headlines, using perfect modals in the passive voice. Make sure each conversation makes sense.

Harvard Professor Claims Egyptian Pyramids Built by Aliens from Outer Space

1. A: Do you think the pyramids .... by aliens from outer space?

B: No way! They .... I just don't believe that!

New Zealand Scientist Argues Dinosaurs Killed by Giant Tsunami

2. A: Do you believe the dinosaurs .... by a giant tsunami?

B: They .... It might explain how they all disappeared so quickly.

SHOCKING NEW REVELATION:
Artist van Gogh was actually murdered by brother

3. A: Do you think van Gogh .... by his brother?

B: Oh, come on! He .... Everyone knows he killed himself.

Woman Attacked by Tiger While Shopping in London

4. A: Do you think someone .... by a tiger in London?

B: Get out of here! That story .... made up!

A: I guess you're right. It ....

PRONUNCIATION BOOSTER ▸ p. P9
• Reduction and linking

NOW YOU CAN *Present a theory about a past event*

A **Frame Your Ideas.** Read about each mystery and the theories explaining it. Which theory do you think is the most possible? Speculate with perfect modals in the passive voice when possible.

Stonehenge

This formation in southern England was built over 3,000 years ago. The stones were brought from mountains far away, but no one knows for sure how the stones were carried or put into place. The purpose for the stone formation is unknown.

Theories:
a. It was used as a type of calendar.
b. It was used for religious ceremonies.
c. It wasn't made or used by people at all—it was formed naturally.

The Nazca Lines

These shapes were carved into the earth in Peru more than 1,500 years ago. However, the people who made them could not have seen what they were carving—the figures can only be seen from an airplane. No one knows how they were made.

Theories:
a. They were carved by ancient people, who used small drawings to design them.
b. With the help of airplanes, they were carved in 1927, right before they were supposedly "discovered."
c. They were created by aliens, who were able to see them from their spaceships.

Atlantis

Around 350 B.C.E., the Greek philosopher Plato wrote about a lost continent called "Atlantis." He describes this advanced civilization in great detail. Researchers argue whether the story is true or comes from Plato's imagination.

Theories:
a. It was a real community established by the Greeks that was destroyed by an earthquake and sank into the ocean.
b. It was a real place discovered by ancient explorers. We know it today as Iceland.
c. Plato was tricked into believing the story by one of his students.

B **Use the Grammar.** Choose one of the mysteries. Present the theory that you think best explains the mystery and tell the class why you believe it.

> *"I believe the stones **may have been used** for religious purposes. That's what makes the most sense to me."*

3

Discuss how believable a story is

A 🎧 4:08 **Word Skills. Using Adjectives with the Suffix -able.**

> **believable** can be accepted as true because it seems possible
> *The story he told seems believable. He backed it up with a lot of details.*
>
> **debatable** not easy to prove because more than one explanation is possible
> *The cause of the explosion is debatable; experts still disagree.*
>
> **provable** can be shown to be definitely true
> *I don't think your theory will be provable, unless clear evidence can be found.*
>
> **questionable** uncertain, but more likely to be untrue
> *Her convincing account of the events makes his version highly questionable.*
>
> **unsolvable** impossible to prove
> *This mystery may be unsolvable. Everyone who saw what happened is no longer alive.*

B **Word Skills Practice.** Complete each statement, using an adjective with the suffix -able. Use each adjective only once.

1. His story is really _____. I doubt that those things could have really happened.

2. I think she's telling the truth. Her description of the events sounds very _____ to me.

3. It is highly _____ whether "lie-detector" testing should be used as evidence. Experts continue to argue about what the test results really mean.

4. What happened to the dinosaurs is not really _____. There is nothing that can show with certainty what really happened.

5. The mystery of what happened to the famous U.S. pilot Amelia Earhart is most likely _____ since her body and the plane have never been found.

C 🎧 4:09 **Listening. Listen for Main Ideas.** Listen to Part 1 of a historical mystery. What happened to the Russian royal family? What's mysterious about this event?

Russia's Royal Family: An Enduring Mystery

Anna Anderson, who claimed to have been Anastasia

Russia's last royal family: Czar Nicholas II and Empress Alexandra with their children, Olga, Maria, Anastasia, Alexei, and Tatiana.

D 🎧 4:10 **Listening. Listen to Summarize.** Now listen to Part 2. What happened in 1991, and what facts did it seem to prove? Why is it still a mystery?

E **Draw Conclusions.** Complete each statement, according to the listening. Listen to Part 2 again if necessary.

1. The czar's son, Alexei, ...
   a. might have been executed with the rest of the family
   b. must have been executed with the rest of the family

2. Researchers believed that five of the nine bodies discovered in 1991 ....
   a. couldn't have been the royal family
   b. had to have been the royal family

3. Anna Anderson, who claimed to be Anastasia, ...
   a. couldn't have been Anastasia
   b. might have been Anastasia

4. More recently, some scientists believed that the bodies ....
   a. might not have been the czar's family
   b. had to have been the czar's family

NOW YOU CAN   *Discuss how believable a story is*

A **Frame Your Ideas.** Think of things you have done that might surprise your classmates. In groups of three, tell each other about one such experience.

I studied to be an opera singer.

B **Game: To Tell the Truth.** In your group, choose one experience that all three of you will claim as your own. The rest of the class asks members of your group questions in order to determine which of you is telling the truth. Make your stories believable to your classmates.

Finally, after all questions have been asked, the class takes a vote on who they think is telling the truth.

I studied to be an opera singer.

Some ideas for questions

How old were you when you did this?
Where exactly were you?
Were you alone or were other people with you?
What did you learn from the experience?
Your own question: ....

C **Use the Vocabulary.** After each group plays the game, explain why you think some students' stories were more believable than others'.

*"I thought your story was **questionable** because..."*

*"**It was obvious that** you were telling the truth because..."*

GOAL
Evaluate the trustworthiness of news sources

A **Reading Warm-up.** Look at the photos and headings in the magazine article. Are you familiar with either of these stories? What do you know about them?

B 🎧 **Reading.** Read the article. Why do you think so many people believed these stories?

Gerd Heidemann   Konrad Kujau

SPECIAL EDITION

The WORLD'S
Greatest Hoaxes

Although they occurred fifty years apart, both of these spectacular hoaxes took the world by storm.

The Loch Ness Monster Story

Snapshot of the "Loch Ness Monster," published by the *Daily Mail*

It was quite a surprise when London's *Daily Mail* printed a photo in 1933 of a creature in Scotland's Loch Ness, the largest and deepest freshwater lake in the United Kingdom. People had been telling stories about such a creature for over a thousand years. But when a respected London surgeon, Colonel Robert Kenneth Wilson, took this photo, the stories suddenly seemed believable. He claimed that while driving by Loch Ness, he saw something strange in the water and quickly grabbed his camera. The photo he took was seen worldwide and began an increased public interest in the "Loch Ness Monster."

Sixty years later, in November 1993, Christian Spurling told a different story. His stepfather, filmmaker and actor Duke Wetherell, had been hired by the *Daily Mail* to look for evidence of the Loch Ness Monster. But instead, he asked his stepson, Spurling, to make a "monster" with his own hands—from a toy boat. His other son, Ian, took the photo. Then, in order to make the story believable, Wetherell asked the surgeon, Colonel Wilson, to say that he had taken the photo.

The story created so much publicity in 1933 that they decided not to admit the hoax. The true story remained a secret for over sixty years. In the meantime, those who believe there is a creature in the lake, continue to do so.

On your ActiveBook disc: *Reading Glossary* and *Extra Reading Comprehension Questions*

The "Hitler Diaries" Hoax

In 1983, the German magazine *Der Stern* announced that reporter Gerd Heidemann had made an incredible discovery: diaries written by Adolf Hitler. The magazine explained that the diaries had been found by farmers after a Nazi plane crashed in a field in April 1945. *Der Stern* paid almost 10 million marks to a Dr. Fischer, who claimed to have retrieved them.

The discovery caused a lot of excitement. Magazines and newspapers in London and New York rushed to print excerpts from the diaries, and scholars and researchers couldn't wait to get their hands on the material to learn more about the century's most infamous dictator. But some skeptics argued that the story couldn't be true— it was well-known that Hitler didn't like to take notes. Nonetheless, *Der Stern* insisted that the authenticity of the diaries was unquestionable.

However, when experts began to examine them, it became clear that the diaries were fake. It turned out that "Dr. Fischer" was actually Konrad Kujau, an art forger who had written the diaries himself, imitating Hitler's own handwriting. And both he and Heidemann had been putting the money from *Der Stern* into their own bank accounts. Both were sent to prison for fraud.

Interestingly, Kujau made a living selling copies of paintings by the world's greatest artists after he was released from prison.

Information source: en.wikipedia.org

admit =	tell the truth
claim =	say that something is true without proof
evidence =	information that proves that something is true
fake =	not real
a forger =	a person who makes things that aren't authentic, such as copies of famous paintings or money
fraud =	the crime of telling a lie to gain money
a hoax =	a story designed to make people believe something that isn't true
infamous =	well-known for having done something bad or morally evil
a skeptic =	a person who doesn't believe claims easily

C **Confirm Facts.** Discuss how best to complete each statement with names from the article.

The Loch Ness Monster Story

1. .... admitted that the Loch Ness Monster photo was a hoax.

2. The fake Loch Ness Monster was made by ....

3. .... didn't really take the photo of the Loch Ness Monster; the photo was actually taken by ....

4. The Loch Ness Monster hoax was created by ....

The "Hitler Diaries" Hoax

1. .... claimed to have discovered the Hitler Diaries.

2. *Der Stern*'s claim that .... had written the diary was questionable.

3. Konrad Kujau was claiming to be ....

4. The evidence showed that the Hitler Diaries were actually written by ....

5. *Der Stern* paid almost 10 million marks to .... and .... , not to Dr. Fischer.

D **Draw Conclusions.** Discuss the questions.

1. Why do you think the media get fooled by sensational hoaxes? Why do they seem to publish these stories so quickly?

2. Do you think hoaxes should be considered a crime, or are they harmless? Why?

NOW YOU CAN *Evaluate the trustworthiness of news sources*

A **Frame Your Ideas.** Complete the survey with a partner. Which of you do you think is more skeptical? Explain.

Are you a skeptic?

	100%	90%	70%	50%	30%	10%	0%
What percentage of the news you read in the newspaper do you think is true?	○	○	○	○	○	○	○
What percentage of the news you hear on TV or radio do you think is true?	○	○	○	○	○	○	○
What percentage of what politicians say do you think is true?	○	○	○	○	○	○	○
What percentage of what you read on the Internet do you think is true?	○	○	○	○	○	○	○
What percentage of what advertisers say do you think is true?	○	○	○	○	○	○	○
What percentage of what your family says do you think is true?	○	○	○	○	○	○	○

B **Notepadding.** On your notepad, list media news sources from print, radio, TV, or the Internet that you trust and ones that you don't. Give reasons for your choices.

The news sources I trust the most	Some news sources I don't trust
Why?	Why not?

C **Discussion.** Why do you trust some news sources and not others? Do you and your classmates agree on any? How can you determine if the information you read or hear is true or not?

Writing: Write a news article

Avoiding Sentence Fragments

A sentence fragment is a group of words that does not express a complete thought.

Two common fragments are:

- **a dependent clause:** a group of words that contains a subject and a verb but begins with a subordinating conjunction, making it an incomplete thought.

    FRAGMENT: After the banker admitted to fraud.

- **a phrase:** a group of words that does not contain a subject and a verb.

    FRAGMENT: With his help.
    FRAGMENT: At the end of the year.
    FRAGMENT: The man giving the speech.

To correct a sentence fragment, do one of the following:

- Attach the fragment to an independent clause to complete the thought.

    After the banker admitted to fraud, **the bank was closed down.**
    We found the hospital with his help.

- Add a subject and / or a verb to make the fragment into a sentence.

    She graduated at the end of the year.
    The man giving the speech **needs a microphone.**

An independent clause:
- contains a subject and a verb
- expresses a complete thought

A complete sentence:
- starts with a capital letter
- ends with a period
- expresses a complete thought
- needs at least one independent clause

Subordinating conjunctions

after	since
as soon as	unless
because	until
before	when
even though	whenever
if	while

ERROR CORRECTION | Correct the errors.

Benefit to Save Library

Last Wednesday, our town hosted a benefit concert. To help save the old building that used to be the library. Developers announced a plan to tear the building down. Two months ago. Because many people feel a connection to the library. The town decided to raise money to restore the building. The benefit concert was a success. Many local musicians performed, and we raised a lot of money.

A **Prewriting. Generating Ideas with Information Questions.**
A news article usually answers information questions about an event. Think of a recent news event. This will be the topic of your article. On your notepad, write information questions about the topic to help generate ideas.

Topic:

Who?

What?

When?

Where?

Why?

How?

B **Writing.** On a separate sheet of paper, write an article about the event, answering your questions from Prewriting. Try to include as much information as you can. Choose a title that reflects the main idea of your article.

C **Self-Check.**

☐ Did you write any sentence fragments? If so, correct them.

☐ Do you have a clear topic sentence?

☐ Is the article interesting? Could you add any more details?

A 🎧 **Listening.** Listen to the conversations. Then listen to each conversation again and choose
the statement that is closer in meaning to what each person said.

1. The woman said she thought ....
   a. it was possible Bill had overslept
   b. most likely Bill had overslept

2. The woman said she thought ....
   a. it was possible the wallet could be Gina's
   b. it was obvious the wallet was Gina's

3. The man said he thought ....
   a. the president may have been involved in the scandal
   b. the president had clearly been involved in the scandal

4. The man said he thought ....
   a. the story could possibly be a hoax
   b. the story couldn't possibly be true

B Change each sentence from direct to indirect speech.

1. She said, "The job will be completed by Monday."

   ....

2. He told me, "Your parents should take the early flight."

   ....

3. My boss said, "Rita may be interested in visiting the art museum."

   ....

4. The school director told us, "Your children must come to class on time."

   ....

5. The clerk said to him, "Your package can be picked up anytime before 5:00 P.M."

   ....

6. The agent told them, "Your passports have to be renewed by tomorrow."

   ....

C On a separate sheet of paper, write your *own* response to each question, using varying degrees
of certainty. Explain your theory.

1. Do you think Bigfoot is real?

   I suppose it's possible, but I really don't believe it . . .

2. We know that the photograph of the Loch Ness Monster was a hoax, but do you think
   the Loch Ness Monster exists?

3. Do you believe there's something mysterious about the Bermuda Triangle that causes ships
   to disappear?

4. Do you think the damage to the forests in Tunguska was caused by a meteorite?

Your Free Time

GOALS After Unit 10, you will be able to:

1 Explain the benefits of leisure activitie
2 Describe hobbies and other interests
3 Compare your use of leisure time
4 Discuss the risk-taking personality

A **Topic Preview.** Read about these technological advances.
Do you know of any other inventions that didn't achieve their promises?

Does technology always live up to its promises?

The promise
Cars were supposed to make it easy to get away from it all.

The reality
Drivers today spend an average of 101 minutes a day driving. And they spend over 40 hours a year stuck in traffic.

The promise
Television was supposed to bring families closer for quality time together.

The reality
Families spend an average of 170 minutes a day watching TV—a lot more time than they spend talking to each other.

The promise
New household appliances were supposed to increase free time and cut back on time spent doing chores.

The reality
Despite increased spending on "laborsaving" devices, people still spend an average of 23.5 hours a week on housework—the same as people living at the beginning of the 20th century.

Information based on U.S. and Canadian government statistics

B **Express Your Ideas.**

1. In your opinion, what technological advances *do* save us time?

2. With all the laborsaving and timesaving inventions available to us today, why is it that everybody complains about not having enough free time?

C 🎧 4:13 **Sound Bites.** Read and listen to a conversation between two close friends at the office.

ED: I can't take it anymore. This job is really getting to me.

KIM: Hey, sounds like you could use a break.

ED: Are you kidding? I'm up to my ears in paperwork.

KIM: When was the last time you took some time off?

ED: Come to think of it, it's been over a year. I was supposed to take off a few weeks in January, but it just got too busy around here.

KIM: Then it sounds like a little R and R* would do you some good.

ED: You're right. And anyway, I can always bring my laptop along and catch up on my work.

KIM: Listen, leave the laptop at home! You need to just take it easy for a while.

* R and R = rest and relaxation

D **Think and Explain.** Read the conversation again. With a partner, explain the meaning of each of the following statements.

1. "This job is really getting to me."
2. "Are you kidding?"
3. "I'm up to my ears in paperwork."
4. "A little R and R would do you some good."
5. "I can catch up on my work."
6. "You need to just take it easy."

STARTING **POINT**

A **Frame Your Ideas.** How do you usually spend your free time? Check all that apply.

- ☐ I hang out with other people.
- ☐ I spend my time alone.
- ☐ I take it easy.
- ☐ I find something exciting to do.
- ☐ I catch up on the chores I never have time for.
- ☐ I catch up on work.
- ☐ I use my time to learn something new.
- ☐ I sit around and worry about what I need to do.
- ☐ Other: ....

B **Pair Work.** Compare how you spend your free time. Discuss what causes stress in your lives.

> **Use these expressions:**
> _____ really gets to me.
> I'm up to my ears in _____.
> I can't catch up on _____.
> I need to take it easy.

111

1

Explain the benefits of leisure activities

A 🎧 **Conversation Snapshot.** Read and listen. Notice the conversation strategies.

A: I've taken up Go recently. Do you play?

B: No. I've never even heard of it. What's Go?

A: It's a great Japanese game. **Kind of like** chess.

B: **I hate to say this, but** I find chess a little boring.

A: **Well, even so,** you should give it a try. I think it's intellectually stimulating. I'm sure you'd like it.

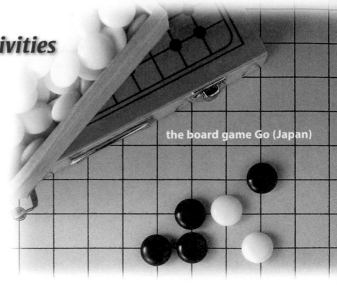
the board game Go (Japan)

🎧 **Rhythm and intonation practice**

B 🎧 **Word Skills. Using Collocations for Leisure Activities.** Add your own game, fitness activity, hobby, or handicraft.

"I play chess."
"I play video games."

Do you **play** any interesting **games**?

Your own game:
....

"I play Ping-Pong."

"I do embroidery."
"I do wood carving."

Do you **do** any **handicrafts**?

Your own handicraft:
....

"I crochet."

"I do karate."
"I do aerobics."

Do you **do** any **fitness activities**?

Your own fitness activity:
....

"I do yoga."

"I raise rabbits."
"I restore antiques."

Do you **have** any **hobbies**?

Your own hobby:
....

"I collect coins."

C **Use Collocations.** First discuss the leisure activities you do or would like to do. Then see which activities are the most popular in your class.

D **Word Skills. Modifying with Adverbs.** Use an adverb to modify a verb or an adjective. Many adverbs are formed by adding -ly to an adjective.

Karate challenges you **physically**. You have to work your body really hard if you want to be good at it. [modifies verb]

I find chess **intellectually** stimulating. You have to use your head to play it well. [modifies adjective]

4:17 🎧 Adjectives	Adverbs
creative	→ **creatively**
emotional	→ **emotionally**
financial	→ **financially**
intellectual	→ **intellectually**
physical	→ **physically**
social	→ **socially**
spiritual	→ **spiritually**

GRAMMAR BOOSTER
▸ p. G16

• Adverbs of manner

E **Word Skills Practice.** Complete the statements with an appropriate adverb. Compare your choices with a partner.

1. Building one-of-a-kind furniture is what makes woodworking so _____ satisfying.

2. While it doesn't feature the punching and kicking found in karate or kung fu, a serious yoga workout can be as _____ difficult as any martial art.

3. Even though there are computer programs that can defeat the greatest chess players, there has never been a program "smart" enough to win the _____ challenging game of Go.

4. They say raising tropical fish can really set you back _____. They're very expensive.

F **Draw Conclusions.** Recommend a leisure activity for each person. Explain your choices.

I've just opened up my own graphic design business. I'm also a full-time mom. Balancing work and family is really challenging. When I do get some free time, I need to do something creative.

Suzy Tanaka

"I think Suzy should take up some kind of handicraft. She might find it relaxing, and it might stimulate her creatively."

I'm a businessperson, and my job is very demanding. Sometimes the stress really gets to me. I have to travel a lot for work—I'm on the go from morning to night. I often get headaches and backaches from all the tension. I really need to get some R and R into my life.

Solange Teixeira

Being a computer programmer, I have to sit at a desk all day long. I work long hours, and by the time I get home at night, I'm pretty exhausted. The only free time I have is on the weekends. But even then, I can't always let go of the job. I've got to find a way to take my mind off of work.

Lionel Espinoza

NOW YOU CAN *Explain the benefits of leisure activities*

A **Frame Your Ideas.** With a partner, discuss and list leisure activities you think fit in each category.

physically challenging	emotionally satisfying	intellectually stimulating	just plain fun!

B **Use the Conversation Strategies.** Talk to your partner about a leisure activity you have taken up or that you would like to try. Explain why you like it. Use the Conversation Snapshot as a guide. Start like this: "I've taken up _____ recently."

GOAL
Describe hobbies and other interests

A 🎧 4:18 **Grammar Snapshot.** Read the message-board posts and notice the noun modifiers.

inter.boards

[ ] [Go]

Does anyone out there have any weird or unusual hobbies or interests?

Back to: INTER Homepage > Message Boards > Hobbies > A weird hobby?

1 2 3 4 of **4** Pages Next > Last >>
Started: Sep 12
Last Post: Nov 16

📝 Post New Message

👆 **A weird hobby?** — Posted Sep 12 4:17AM

Sameer
1 Posts (View)

I have **a weird ten-year-old** hobby that I know no one will ever understand. I like to walk up and down the beach with one of **those silly metal** detectors looking for lost coins and watches. Hey, it keeps me out of trouble.

23 replies, view all [Reply]

❗ **Hobbies can be obsessive.** — Posted Sep 17 11:45AM

Eric B.
5 Posts (View)

Too much time on your hands, Sameer? LOL*! Actually, I'm **an obsessive comic book** collector. It's just this thing I've been into since I was a teenager.

1 reply, view all [Reply]

👆 **My hobby takes all my time!** — Posted Sep 18 2:12PM

Susieq
1 Posts (View)

Speaking of obsessions, mine is knitting. Really, I can't stop! **Six-foot-long** scarves, **thick multicolored** sweaters, **cute little teapot** warmers. . . . I keep churning them out whether my friends and family want them or not!

1 reply, view all [Reply]

*LOL = laughing out loud

B **Grammar. Order of modifiers**

When a noun is modified by more than one word, modifiers usually appear in the following order.

❶ **determiners**: a, an, the, this, my, Judy's
❷ **ordinals**: first, one thousandth
❸ **quantifiers**: one, a few, some, many
❹ **adjectives** (in the following order):
   size: small, huge, tall, wide
   an opinion or quality: beautiful, clear, weird, obsessive
   age or temperature: young, middle-aged, antique, freezing
   shape: round, triangular
   color: black, greenish
   origin: British, handmade
   material: glass, silk, metal
❺ **nouns**: student, childhood, book, teapot

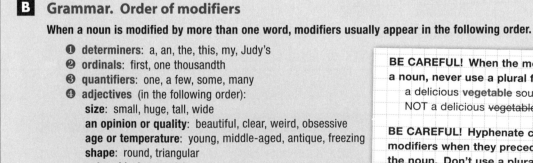

my first few beautiful antique Czech crystal sugar bowls
❶ ❷ ❸ ❹ ❺

> **BE CAREFUL!** When the modifier is a noun, never use a plural form.
> a delicious **vegetable** soup
> NOT a delicious ~~vegetables~~ soup
>
> **BE CAREFUL!** Hyphenate compound modifiers when they precede the noun. Don't use a plural form.
> a **two-year-old** house
> NOT a two-~~years~~-old house
> BUT The house is two years old.

GRAMMAR BOOSTER ▸ p. G16
• Intensifiers

Identify Supporting Details. Discuss the questions.

1. The author states that advances in technology such as e-[mail and the]
   Internet are "destroying any idea of privacy and leisure." [How do these]
   technologies do that in his view? Give specific examples[.]

2. The author states that "technology almost never does wh[at...]
   people have each time a new technology appears? Give [examples.]

3. Do you agree with the author's point of view in the artic[le?]

NOW YOU CAN *Compare your use of leisure*

A **Frame Your Ideas.** Complete the survey. Then circle the activit[ies...]

Check how frequently you do each

	Very often	Frequently
running errands	◯	◯
doing housework	◯	◯
surfing the Web	◯	◯
catching up on personal e-mail	◯	◯
keeping in touch with friends by telephone	◯	◯
spending time with family	◯	◯
attending cultural events	◯	◯
working on a hobby or interest	◯	◯
playing games (video, board games, sports)	◯	◯
reading for pleasure	◯	◯
listening to music	◯	◯
watching TV	◯	◯
exercising	◯	◯
taking naps	◯	◯
eating out	◯	◯
other:	◯	◯

B **Make Personal Comparisons.** With a partner, compare how yo[u spend]
your time. Which activities do you wish you spent more time on?
Are there any you think you spend too much time on?

C **Discussion.** In what ways does technology
add to or interfere with your leisure time? What can
you do to keep work or study balanced with leisure
time in your life?

> "E-mail kee[ps...]
> I don't thin[k...]"

C **Grammar Practice.** On a separate sheet of paper, rewrite each sentence, correcting the order of the noun modifiers. Explain your corrections.

> "Opinions come before colors."

1. Are you going to wear that green ugly cotton shirt?
2. That was the most interesting French old film I've ever seen.
3. I gave her a wooden beautiful round box that I picked up during my trip.
4. She bought an Italian hundred-year-old expensive violin.
5. Isn't this the third mystery historical novel you've read this month?
6. He bought her a silk white gorgeous handkerchief.

D **Grammar Practice.** Complete the sentences with compound modifiers, using the descriptions in parentheses.

1. She bought a new .... bike.
   (It has ten speeds.)

2. They offer a .... introductory class at the new yoga school.
   (It runs for three months.)

3. We gave her a small .... pillow.
   (It was embroidered by hand.)

4. The company sent him a .... letter.
   (It was filled with praise.)

5. The government announced a .... plan for protecting
   (It has five points.)
   the environment.

NOW YOU CAN *Describe hobbies and other interests*

A **Notepadding.** Think of some things you and people you know like to do or make. On your notepad, write sentences about these hobbies or interests, using at least three noun modifiers to describe each.

> I've been collecting beautiful antique handmade paper dolls for years.
> My sister has always liked to watch old black-and-white Hollywood movies.

B **Use the Grammar.** Walk around the classroom and interview your classmates about the hobbies and interests they wrote about on their notepads. Then tell your class about the most interesting hobbies or interests you heard about, using noun modifiers.

3 GOAL
Compare your use of leisure time

A Reading Warm-up. Are you satisfied with the amount of

B 🎧 Reading. Read the article. What's the author's main p

IS TECHNOLOGY LEISURE TIME?

by Jo

New surveys suggest that the technological tools we use to make our lives easier are killing our leisure time. We are working longer hours, taking fewer and shorter vacations (and when we do go away, we take our cell phones, PDAs, and laptops along). And we are more stressed than ever as increased use of e-mail, voice mail, cell phones, and the Internet are destroying any idea of privacy and leisure.

Since the Industrial Revolution, people have assumed that new laborsaving devices would free them from the burdens of the workplace and give them more time to grow intellectually, creatively, and socially— exploring the arts, keeping up with current events, spending more time with friends and family, and even just "goofing off."

But here we are at the start of the 21st century, enjoying one of the greatest technological boom times in human history, and nothing could be further from the truth. The very tools that were supposed to liberate us have bound us to our work and study in ways that were inconceivable just a few years ago. It would seem that technology almost never does what we expect.

In "the old days," the lin work and leisure time w clearer. People left their a predictable time, were completely disconnected out of touch with their they traveled to and fr and were off-duty onc home. That's no long today's highly compe market, employers d increased productivi workers to put in l hours and to keep almost constantly cell phones, e-mail communications devices. employees feel the need on what's going on at th on days off. They feel pr work after hours just to everything they have to work harder and longer, work tasks more frequen more and more reasons t about job security.

Bosses, colleagues, and fa members—lovers, friends spouses too—expect insta responses to voice mail ar messages. Even college st have become bound to th desks by an environment in which faculty, friends, and other members of the college

On your ActiveBook disc: *Reading Glossary* and *Extra Reading Comprehension Questions*

---

4 GOAL
Discuss the risk-taking personality

Do people who ride roller coasters have a "big T" or "small t" personality?

A 🎧 Listening. Listen to Define. Listen to the interview with a psychologist. Then listen again and write a description for each of the two personality types the psychologist describes.

What is a "big T" personality?	What is a "small t" personality?

B Relate to Personal Experience. Where do you fit on the risk-taking continuum? Do you have a "big T" or a "small t" personality? Give examples to support your opinion.

◄ RISK-TAKER   RISK-AVOIDER ►

C 🎧 Vocabulary. Ways to Express Fear and Fearlessness. Listen and practice.

I can't wait to go hang gliding.

I wouldn't dare go hang gliding.

Skydiving doesn't scare me a bit.

Skydiving scares the life out of me.

There's nothing like surfing.

There's not a chance I would go surfing.

I can't get enough of white-water rafting.

You wouldn't catch me white-water rafting.

You'd have to be out of your mind to go bungee jumping.

Bungee jumping is no sweat.

PRONUNCIATION BOOSTER ▸ p. P10
• Vowel sounds

D **Vocabulary Practice.** With a partner, use the Vocabulary to discuss which extreme sports you would or would not be willing to do.

"Rock climbing **scares the life out of me.**"

surfing

rock climbing

mountain biking

extreme skiing

skydiving

waterfall jumping

NOW YOU CAN *Discuss the risk-taking personality*

A **Notepadding.** What's the riskiest thing your partner has ever done? Interview him or her and take notes on your notepad. Where would *you* place your partner on the risk-taking continuum?

What?	Other details:
Where?	
When?	
How?	

B **Make Comparisons.** In small groups, compare your partners' experiences. Then decide who is the most fearless.

C **Discussion.**

1. In your opinion, why does one person develop into a risk-taker and another into a risk-avoider?

2. Do you think risk-taking is a healthy type of behavior? Where do you think the best place to be on the risk-taking continuum is? Why?

Writing: *Comment on another's point of view*

Expressing and Supporting Opinions Clearly

When you write to critique or comment on another's spoken or written ideas, present your reasons logically, using connecting words to give reasons and to sequence your ideas.

Giving reasons

People have more free time **since** they are able to work from home.

Because of the Internet, people are working more efficiently.

Actually, using new technology doesn't save paper. **This is why** I think the author is wrong.

Due to new technological advances, working at home has become easier than ever.

Sequencing ideas

First of all, I agree with Jon Katz's main point.

I **also** think he makes a good point about modern technology.

In addition, I think he's right about technology in the workplace.

Finally, we need to decide what we want technology to do for us.

WRITING MODEL

I disagree with almost all of Jon Katz's ideas in his article "Is Technology Killing Leisure Time?" **since** most new inventions actually help us increase the time we have for leisure activities. **First of all,** when Katz says, "Technology almost never does what we expect," he is ignoring the popularity of most new technologies. If a technology did not achieve its promise, it would not be so popular. **In addition,** I

A Prewriting. Developing Arguments.

Read the article "Is Technology Killing Leisure Time?" on page 116 and underline sentences that you agree with or do not agree with. On a separate sheet of paper, do the following:

- paraphrase each sentence you underlined
- provide the reasons why you agree or disagree

Quoting the author

You can write short statements in direct speech using quotes, as shown in the Writing Model. Paraphrase longer statements in indirect speech.

> The author says that technology almost never does what we expect.
> I disagree because it isn't true for most new inventions. The popularity of most new technologies proves that people are happy with them.

B Writing.

On a separate sheet of paper, write a critique of the article. State your own opinion at the beginning. Use the sentences you underlined and the comments you wrote to support your opinion.

C Self-Check.

- ☐ Is your opinion clearly stated?
- ☐ Did you use connecting words to support your reasons and sequence your ideas?
- ☐ Did you use quotation marks when using the author's own words?
- ☐ Did you paraphrase the author's words when you didn't use direct speech?

A 🎧 **Listening.** Listen to the conversations about free time. Infer the kind of leisure activity the people are discussing.

1. ☐ a game ☐ a fitness activity ☐ a hobby ☐ a handicraft
2. ☐ a game ☐ a fitness activity ☐ a hobby ☐ a handicraft
3. ☐ a game ☐ a fitness activity ☐ a hobby ☐ a handicraft
4. ☐ a game ☐ a fitness activity ☐ a hobby ☐ a handicraft

B Categorize the leisure activities in the box. Use a dictionary for words you don't know. Add other activities.

hobbies	games	handicrafts	fitness activities

collecting stamps	lifting weights
making jewelry	sewing
playing checkers	doing puzzles
doing tae kwon do	knitting
playing cards	restoring old cars
growing roses	raising iguanas

C Use the words in the box to modify the nouns. Use at least three modifiers for each noun.

a / an	this / that	his / her	new	intelligent	English
some	many	green	stylish	black	handmade
adorable	destructive	sincere	clever	antique	South American
flashy	young	small	cotton	friendly	law

1. .... sweater
2. .... parrot
3. .... student
4. .... teacup

D Complete the statements in your *own* way.

1. .... scares the life out of me.
2. You'd have to be out of your mind to ....
3. You wouldn't catch me ....
4. .... doesn't scare me a bit.
5. I can't wait to ....
6. There's nothing like ....

Pronunciation table

These are the pronunciation symbols used in *Summit 1*.

Vowels

Symbol	Key Word	Symbol	Key Word
i	beat, feed	ə	banana, among
ɪ	bit, did	ɚ	shirt, murder
eɪ	date, paid	aɪ	bite, cry, buy, eye
ɛ	bet, bed	aʊ	about, how
æ	bat, bad	ɔɪ	voice, boy
ɑ	box, odd, father	ɪr	beer
ɔ	bought, dog	ɛr	bare
oʊ	boat, road	ɑr	bar
ʊ	book, good	ɔr	door
u	boot, food, student	ʊr	tour
ʌ	but, mud, mother		

Consonants

Symbol	Key Word	Symbol	Key Word
p	pack, happy	z	zip, please, goes
b	back, rubber	ʃ	ship, machine, station, special, discussion
t	tie		
d	die		
k	came, key, quick	ʒ	measure, vision
g	game, guest	h	hot, who
tʃ	church, nature, watch	m	men, some
dʒ	judge, general, major	n	sun, know, pneumonia
f	fan, photograph	ŋ	sung, ringing
v	van	w	wet, white
θ	thing, breath	l	light, long
ð	then, breathe	r	right, wrong
s	sip, city, psychology	y	yes, use, music
		t̬	butter, bottle
		t˺	button

Irregular verbs

base form	simple past	past participle	base form	simple past	past participle
be	was / were	been	forget	forgot	forgotten
beat	beat	beaten	forgive	forgave	forgiven
become	became	become	freeze	froze	frozen
begin	began	begun	get	got	gotten
bend	bent	bent	give	gave	given
bet	bet	bet	go	went	gone
bite	bit	bitten	grow	grew	grown
bleed	bled	bled	hang	hung	hung
blow	blew	blown	have	had	had
break	broke	broken	hear	heard	heard
breed	bred	bred	hide	hid	hidden
bring	brought	brought	hit	hit	hit
build	built	built	hold	held	held
burn	burned / burnt	burned / burnt	hurt	hurt	hurt
burst	burst	burst	keep	kept	kept
buy	bought	bought	know	knew	known
catch	caught	caught	lay	laid	laid
choose	chose	chosen	lead	led	led
come	came	come	leap	leaped / leapt	leaped / leapt
cost	cost	cost	learn	learned / learnt	learned / learnt
creep	crept	crept	leave	left	left
cut	cut	cut	lend	lent	lent
deal	dealt	dealt	let	let	let
dig	dug	dug	lie	lay	lain
do	did	done	light	lit	lit
draw	drew	drawn	lose	lost	lost
dream	dreamed / dreamt	dreamed / dreamt	make	made	made
drink	drank	drunk	mean	meant	meant
drive	drove	driven	meet	met	met
eat	ate	eaten	mistake	mistook	mistaken
fall	fell	fallen	pay	paid	paid
feed	fed	fed	put	put	put
feel	felt	felt	quit	quit	quit
fight	fought	fought	read /rid/	read /rɛd/	read /rɛd/
find	found	found	ride	rode	ridden
fit	fit	fit	ring	rang	rung
fly	flew	flown	rise	rose	risen
forbid	forbade	forbidden	run	ran	run

base form	simple past	past participle	base form	simple past	past participle
say	said	said	spring	sprang / sprung	sprung
see	saw	seen	stand	stood	stood
sell	sold	sold	steal	stole	stolen
send	sent	sent	stick	stuck	stuck
set	set	set	sting	stung	stung
shake	shook	shaken	stink	stank / stunk	stunk
shed	shed	shed	strike	struck	struck / stricken
shine	shone	shone	string	strung	strung
shoot	shot	shot	swear	swore	sworn
show	showed	shown	sweep	swept	swept
shrink	shrank	shrunk	swim	swam	swum
shut	shut	shut	swing	swung	swung
sing	sang	sung	take	took	taken
sink	sank	sunk	teach	taught	taught
sit	sat	sat	tear	tore	torn
sleep	slept	slept	tell	told	told
slide	slid	slid	think	thought	thought
smell	smelled / smelt	smelled / smelt	throw	threw	thrown
speak	spoke	spoken	understand	understood	understood
speed	sped / speeded	sped / speeded	upset	upset	upset
spell	spelled / spelt	spelled / spelt	wake	woke / waked	woken / waked
spend	spent	spent	wear	wore	worn
spill	spilled / spilt	spilled / spilt	weave	wove	woven
spin	spun	spun	weep	wept	wept
spit	spit / spat	spit / spat	win	won	won
spoil	spoiled / spoilt	spoiled / spoilt	wind	wound	wound
spread	spread	spread	write	wrote	written

Stative verbs

amaze	desire	hear	need	seem
appear*	dislike	imagine	owe	smell*
appreciate	doubt	include*	own	sound
astonish	envy	know	please	suppose
be*	equal	like	possess	surprise
believe	exist	look like	prefer	taste*
belong	fear	look*	realize	think*
care	feel*	love	recognize	understand
consist of	forget	matter	remember*	want*
contain	hate	mean	resemble	weigh*
cost	have*	mind	see*	

*These verbs also have action meanings. Example: *I see a tree.* (non-action) *I'm seeing her tomorrow.* (action)

Verbs followed by a gerund

acknowledge	consider	endure	imagine	prevent	resent
admit	delay	enjoy	justify	prohibit	resist
advise	deny	escape	keep	propose	risk
appreciate	detest	explain	mention	quit	suggest
avoid	discontinue	feel like	mind	recall	support
can't help	discuss	finish	miss	recommend	tolerate
celebrate	dislike	forgive	postpone	report	understand
complete	don't mind	give up	practice		

Expressions that can be followed by a gerund

be excited about	be opposed to	believe in	blame [someone or something] for
be worried about	be used to	participate in	forgive [someone or something] for
be responsible for	complain about	succeed in	thank [someone or something] for
be interested in	dream about / of	take advantage of	keep [someone or something] from
be accused of	talk about / of	take care of	prevent [someone or something] from
be capable of	think about / of	insist on	stop [someone or something] from
be tired of	apologize for	look forward to	
be accustomed to	make an excuse for		
be committed to	have a reason for		

Verbs followed directly by an infinitive

afford	choose	grow	mean	pretend	threaten
agree	claim	hesitate	need	promise	volunteer
appear	consent	hope	neglect	refuse	wait
arrange	decide	hurry	offer	request	want
ask	demand	intend	pay	seem	wish
attempt	deserve	learn	plan	struggle	would like
can't wait	expect	manage	prepare	swear	yearn
care	fail				

Verbs followed by an object before an infinitive*

advise	choose*	force	need*	remind	urge
allow	convince	get*	order	request	want*
ask*	enable	help*	pay	require	warn
beg	encourage	hire	permit	teach	wish*
cause	expect*	instruct	persuade	tell	would like*
challenge	forbid	invite	promise*		

*In the active voice, these verbs can be followed by the infinitive without an object (example: *want to speak* or *want someone to speak*).

Adjectives followed by an infinitive*

afraid	content	disturbed	glad	proud	sorry
alarmed	curious	eager	happy	ready	surprised
amazed	delighted	easy	hesitant	relieved	touched
angry	depressed	embarrassed	likely	reluctant	upset
anxious	determined	encouraged	lucky	sad	willing
ashamed	disappointed	excited	pleased	shocked	
certain	distressed	fortunate	prepared		

*Example: *I'm willing **to accept** that.*

Verbs that can be followed by a gerund or an infinitive

with a change in meaning

forget (+ gerund)	=	forget something that happened
(+ infinitive)	=	forget something that needs to be done
regret (+ gerund)	=	regret a past action
(+ infinitive)	=	regret having to inform someone about an action
remember (+ gerund)	=	remember something that happened
(+ infinitive)	=	remember something that needs to be done
stop (+ gerund)	=	stop a continuous action
(+ infinitive)	=	stop in order to do something

without a change in meaning

begin	love
can't stand	prefer
continue	start
hate	try
like	

Participial adjectives

alarming	–	alarmed	disturbing	–	disturbed	paralyzing	–	paralyzed
amazing	–	amazed	embarrassing	–	embarrassed	pleasing	–	pleased
amusing	–	amused	entertaining	–	entertained	relaxing	–	relaxed
annoying	–	annoyed	exciting	–	excited	satisfying	–	satisfied
astonishing	–	astonished	exhausting	–	exhausted	shocking	–	shocked
boring	–	bored	fascinating	–	fascinated	soothing	–	soothed
comforting	–	comforted	frightening	–	frightened	startling	–	startled
confusing	–	confused	horrifying	–	horrified	stimulating	–	stimulated
depressing	–	depressed	inspiring	–	inspired	surprising	–	surprised
disappointing	–	disappointed	interesting	–	interested	terrifying	–	terrified
disgusting	–	disgusted	irritating	–	irritated	tiring	–	tired
distressing	–	distressed	moving	–	moved	touching	–	touched

Grammar Booster

The *Grammar Booster* is optional. It provides more explanation and practice as well as additional grammar concepts.

Unit 1

Gerunds and infinitives: summary

Gerunds

A gerund functions as a noun. A gerund or gerund phrase can be the subject of a sentence, a direct or indirect object, a subject complement, or the object of a preposition.

Living a balanced life is about integrating all parts of it. [subject]
I love spending time with my family. [direct object]
The best part of life is learning new things. [subject complement]
Here are some tips for getting a healthy perspective on life. [object of a preposition]

Infinitives

An infinitive also functions as a noun. An infinitive or infinitive phrase can be the subject of a sentence, but infinitives as subjects are often considered awkward. It is more common to use an impersonal It as the subject.

To be honest isn't always easy. [subject]
OR It isn't always easy to be honest.

An infinitive or infinitive phrase can be a direct object or a subject complement.

I want to feel less stressed. [direct object]
My favorite thing is to spend time with friends. [subject complement]

An infinitive or infinitive phrase can express a purpose.

Make time to relax.
We stopped to buy some gas.

> ### REMEMBER
>
> **Some verbs can only be followed by a gerund.**
> I suggest asking her if she can make it.
> We finished writing the report.
> He recommends not waiting till the last minute.
>
> **Some verbs can only be followed by an infinitive.**
> You should expect to be there by early afternoon.
> I hope to complete the course.
> Learn not to live in the past.
>
> **Some verbs can be followed by a gerund or an infinitive with no change in meaning.**
> He likes listening to jazz.
> He likes to listen to jazz.
>
> **Some verbs require an object before an infinitive.**
> He reminded me to call my mother.
> I persuaded them not to sell their house.
> The school permitted her to skip the first level.
>
> **Some adjectives can be followed by an infinitive.**
> He was surprised to get the promotion.
> I was disappointed to hear the news.
>
> **For a complete list of verbs, adjectives, and expressions followed by gerunds and infinitives, see pages A3–A4 in the Appendices.**

A Complete each sentence with a gerund or infinitive form of the verb. Refer to pages A3–A4 in the Appendices if necessary.

1. We were delighted _____ out that we had won the contest.
   (find)

2. Be sure to thank your father for _____ me get that interview.
   (help)

3. She goes to the gym five times a week _____ in shape.
   (stay)

4. Don't be surprised if he refuses _____ with them.
   (cooperate)

5. _____ other people for help is sometimes hard to do.
   (ask)

6. They definitely won't permit you _____ that on board.
   (carry)

B On a separate sheet of paper, rewrite the following sentences, using an impersonal It as the subject of the sentence.

1. To pass the examination is not the easiest thing in the world.
2. To speak English fluently is my greatest wish.
3. To live in an English-speaking country might be an exciting experience.
4. To know when to use an infinitive and when to use a gerund is pretty confusing.

Grammar for Writing: parallelism with gerunds and infinitives

A common error in formal written English is mixing gerunds and infinitives when listing items in a series. A list of items should either be all gerunds or all infinitives.

When I take time off from work, I prefer **relaxing** at home, **spending** time with my family, and **getting** things done around the house.

NOT I prefer relaxing at home, spending time with my family, and ~~to get~~ things done around the house.

I can't stand **getting up** late and **missing** the bus.

NOT I can't stand getting up late and ~~to miss~~ the bus.

In a series, either use <u>to</u> with all the infinitives or only with the first one.

When I take time off from work, I prefer **to relax** at home, **spend** time with my family, and **get** things done around the house.

NOT When I take time off from work, I prefer to relax at home, spend time with my family, and ~~to~~ get things done around the house.

C On a separate sheet of paper, correct the errors in parallelism in the following sentences.

1. After she arrived in London, she began to write long letters home and calling her parents at all hours of the night.

2. There are two things I really can't stand doing: speaking in front of large audiences and chat with people I don't know at parties.

3. Right before midnight, everyone began to sing, dance, and to welcome in the new year.

4. There's no question I prefer using all my vacation time and take a long vacation.

D Complete the following sentences, using appropriate gerund or infinitive forms. Refer to pages A3–A4 in the Appendices if necessary.

1. I would suggest .... out the form immediately and .... a copy for
   (fill)   (make)
   your records.

2. Did you remember .... off the stove, ... the windows, and
   (turn)   (close)
   .... the door before you left?
   (lock)

3. It's obvious from her e-mails that she really loves .... the culture, ...
   (experience)   (meet)
   new people, and just .... there.
   (be)

4. They prohibit .... photographs or .... a recorder.
   (take)   (use)

5. I really wouldn't mind .... them out to dinner or .... them
   (take)   (show)
   around if you'd like me to.

6. He promised .... the report home, ... it carefully, and ....
   (take)   (read)   (respond)
   to any questions by the next day.

Unit 2

Finished and unfinished actions: summary

Finished actions

Use the simple past tense or the past of <u>be</u> for an action finished at a specified time in the past.
> They **watched** that DVD yesterday.

Use the present perfect for an action finished at an unspecified time in the past.
> They**'ve watched** that DVD three times.

Use the past perfect for an action that was finished before another action in the past.
> When I arrived, they **had** already **watched** the DVD.

NOTE: Although the continuous aspect is used for actions in progress, the present perfect continuous is sometimes used for very recently completed actions, especially to emphasize duration.
> They**'ve been watching** that DVD all afternoon, but they're done now.

Unfinished actions

Use the present perfect OR the present perfect continuous for unfinished actions that began in the past and may continue into the future. Use the present perfect continuous to further emphasize that the action is continuous.
> She**'s listened** to Ray Charles for years. [And she may continue.]
> OR She**'s been listening** to Ray Charles for years. [And she may continue.]

A Complete the article, using the simple past tense, the past of <u>be</u>, or the present perfect.

World Music is not really a true genre of music—it is a combination of musical genres from around the

world. For a number of years, recording companies .... the term to describe the music of artists who
(1. use)

they feel could appeal to new audiences across cultures. The concept of World Music .... first created
(2. be)

after U.S. singer / songwriter Paul Simon .... his hugely successful *Graceland* album in 1986. At that
(3. record)

time, he .... South Africa's male choir Ladysmith Black Mambazo and rock group Savuka to accompany
(4. invite)

him on the recording. Both groups later .... with him around the world. This exciting collaboration
(5. tour)

immediately .... to European and North American audiences, who were attracted to this different sound.
(6. appeal)

Since that time, as more artists .... to reach new audiences, there .... an increased amount
(7. try)   (8. be)

of "crossover"—that is, musicians influencing each other across cultures. Enthusiasm for music from other cultures

.... steadily. Artists such as Angélique Kidjo and Carlos Vives, who were well-known within specific
(9. rise)

regions such as Africa or Latin America, ... international stars, and mainstream music ....
(10. become)   (11. incorporate)

many of the features of these artists.

B Read each statement. Then decide which description is closer in meaning.

1. By the time I heard about it, the concert had sold out.
   a. First I heard about the concert. Then it sold out.
   b. First the concert sold out. Then I heard about it.

2. After he'd won the award, he got a big recording contract.
   a. First he got the recording contract. Then he won the award.
   b. First he won the award. Then he got the recording contract.

3. We wanted to go to his performance because we'd heard his new CD.
   a. First we heard his CD. Then we wanted to go to his performance.
   b. First we wanted to go to his performance. Then we heard his CD.

4. He'd played at a lot of different halls before he performed at Carnegie Hall.
   a. First he performed at Carnegie Hall. Then he played at a lot of different halls.
   b. First he played at a lot of different halls. Then he performed at Carnegie Hall.

The past perfect continuous

Use the past perfect continuous for a continuous action that occurred and finished before an earlier time or event.

By 1998, he **had been studying** French for about five years.

When the test began, the students **had been waiting** for over an hour.

NOTE: This structure tends to occur more in formal writing than in speaking.

C Use the present perfect continuous or the past perfect continuous to complete each statement.

1. Stella is such a big fan of Bob Marley that she .... nothing but his recordings for years.
(collect)

2. Jill Morsberger .... at clubs for ten years before Greenwood Entertainment invited her
(perform)
to sign a recording contract.

3. Jeff .... at the airport for his girlfriend when he saw the lead singer for U2.
(wait)

4. She must be extremely popular. The audience .... in line to buy tickets for over two
(stand)
hours.

5. The lead guitarist for the band .... the new songs for weeks. That's why they sound
(rehearse)
so good tonight.

6. Shakira .... songs only in Spanish before she decided to branch out and try recording
(record)
songs in English for the U.S. market.

Grammar for Writing: noun clauses as adjective and noun complements

Noun clauses as subjects are awkward and generally avoided.
Two ways to rewrite such sentences follow.

Use a noun clause as an adjective complement.

AVOIDED **That Frankel is quite critical of modern art** is obvious.
PREFERRED It is obvious **(that) Frankel is quite critical of modern art**.

Use a noun clause as a noun complement.

AVOIDED **That her job was so difficult** was why she quit.
PREFERRED The fact **that her job was so difficult** was why she quit.

Impersonal expressions that introduce noun clauses

It is **important** (that)
It appears **obvious** (that)
It seems **clear** (that)
It becomes **essential** (that)
It is **possible** (that)
It looks **likely** (that)

Noun phrases that can precede a noun clause

the **announcement** that	the **news** that
the **argument** that	the **possibility** that
the **belief** that	the **proposal** that
the **chance** that	the **reason** that
the **claim** that	the **recommendation** that
the **demand** that	the **report** that
the **fact** that	the **suggestion** that
the **idea** that	

The reason that she refuses to appear in films is a mystery to everyone.

The argument that classical music is dead makes no sense.

The news that the new CEO is retiring surprised a lot of people.

D On a separate sheet of paper, rewrite each sentence, using the impersonal <u>It</u>.

1. That developing countries address the problems caused by global warming is extremely important.
2. That the president plans on resigning appears obvious to everyone.
3. That not providing disaster relief will only worsen the situation seems quite clear.
4. That a cure for cancer will be discovered in the next twenty years is certainly possible.
5. That the governments of Argentina and Chile will reach an agreement looks very likely.
6. That Max Bianchi won't be participating in the Olympics next year is not important.

E Read each quote from a radio news program. Then, on a separate sheet of paper, complete each statement, using the noun clause as a noun complement.

Example: "Volkswagen announced that they would unveil a new car design early next year. This is causing a lot of excitement in the auto industry." [The announcement . . .]

> *The announcement that Volkswagen would unveil a new car design early next year is causing a lot of excitement in the auto industry.*

1. "The Health Ministry announced that they will begin vaccinating all infants for measles. This was greeted with criticism from the opposition party." [The announcement . . .]
2. "The president said it was possible that he would resign by the end of this year. This has taken everyone by surprise, including the news media." [The possibility . . .]
3. "The *London Sun* reported that Dr. Regina Blair of the Glasgow Medical Center has discovered a new protein. This is attracting much interest in the world of science." [The report . . .]
4. "The *Auckland Times* claimed that a 95-year-old New Zealand man had broken the world record for growing the longest beard. This has triggered similar claims across three continents." [The claim . . .]

Unit 3

The future continuous

Use the future continuous for actions that will be in progress at a specific time or over a period of time in the future.
To form the future continuous, use <u>will</u> + <u>be</u> + a present participle OR <u>be going to</u> + <u>be</u> + a present participle.

At this time next week, I { **'ll be lying** / **'m going to be lying** } on a beach in Hawaii. [specific time]

I { **'ll be studying** / **'m going to be studying** } English in the United States for about two years. [period of time]

REMEMBER

Stative verbs are "non-action" verbs such as <u>be</u>, <u>have</u>, <u>know</u>, <u>remember</u>, <u>like</u>, <u>seem</u>, <u>appreciate</u>, etc.

Do not use the continuous with stative verbs.
DON'T SAY By next month, I~~'ll be having~~ a new car.

For a complete list of stative verbs, see page A3 in the Appendices.

Sometimes sentences in the simple future and the future continuous have almost the same meaning. Choose the future continuous to emphasize a continuous or uninterrupted activity.
Next year, I'll **study** English in the United States.
Next year, I'll **be studying** English in the United States.

Questions and short answers
Will you **be working** at home? Yes, I will. / No, I won't.
Are you **going to be working** at home? Yes, I am. / No, I'm not.

Use the future continuous and a time clause with <u>while</u> or <u>when</u> to describe a continuous activity that will occur at the same time as another activity. Do not use a future form in the time clause.
I'll **be looking** for a job while my wife **continues** her studies.
NOT I'll be looking for a job while my wife ~~will be continuing~~ her studies.

When the mayor **is speaking**, we'll **be listening** carefully.
NOT When the mayor ~~will be speaking~~, we'll be listening carefully.

A On a separate sheet of paper, correct the errors in the following sentences.

1. She'll be staying at the Newton Hotel when she's going to be attending the meeting.
2. We won't be spending much time sightseeing while we'll be visiting London.
3. When he's going to stay in town, he's going to be meeting with some friends.
4. She'll be correcting homework while the students will be taking the test.
5. While Michelle will be serving dessert, Randy will already be washing the dishes.
6. Won't they be going to sleep in New York when you'll be getting up in Taipei?

B Complete the following sentences, using the future continuous with <u>will</u> when possible. If the future continuous is not possible, use the simple future with <u>will</u>.

1. After I've completed my studies, I _____ for a job.
   (look)

2. She _____ historic sites while she's in Turkey.
   (photograph)

3. In a few years, they _____ all the problems they had.
   (not / remember)

4. _____ he _____ between flights for very long?
   (wait)

5. I'm sure she _____ when you call.
   (not / sleep)

The future perfect continuous

Use the future perfect continuous to emphasize the continuous quality of an action that began before a specific time in the future. To form the future perfect continuous, use <u>will</u> + <u>have</u> + <u>been</u> and a present participle.

By next year, I**'ll have been studying** English for five years. [Describes an action that began before "next year" and may still continue.]

Combine a statement using the future perfect continuous with a time clause to show the relationship between two future actions. Use the simple present tense in the time clause.

By the time I **arrive** in New York, I**'ll have been sitting** in a plane for over ten hours.
NOT By the time I~~'ll arrive~~ in New York, I'll have been sitting in a plane for over ten hours.

C Complete the notecard, using the future continuous or the future perfect continuous.

Dear Iaa,

Venice was great, but finally on to Paris! By tomorrow afternoon, I _____ down
(1. stroll)
the Champs Elysées and _____ in
(2. take)
the beautiful sights of that great city. In the evening, I _____ an opera by Bizet
(3. enjoy)
in the city where he was born. Just think, by Saturday, I _____ delicious French
(4. eat)
food for a whole week! Plus, I _____
(5. practice)
my French with real native speakers.

Then, after Paris, it's off to the Riviera, where I _____ around on the beaches of
(6. lounge)
Nice and Saint-Tropez for a week. By that time, I _____ for three weeks, and it will
(7. travel)
almost be time to come home—a long trip for a homebody like me!

See you soon!

Pavel

Unit 4

A **Review.** Check *all* the quantifiers that can complete each sentence correctly.

1. If a child watches _____ television, he or she may develop a self-image problem.
   ☐ a lot of ☐ several ☐ a number of ☐ a great deal of

2. I don't think you can say that _____ young people are self-conscious about their bodies.
   ☐ most ☐ a great deal of ☐ every ☐ a majority of

3. It's clear that _____ company needs to make its own decision about it.
   ☐ some ☐ each ☐ every ☐ most

4. There are _____ beauty treatments available to our customers.
   ☐ a number of ☐ a few ☐ plenty of ☐ a little

5. I was surprised to read that _____ men are considering cosmetic surgery.
   ☐ a lot of ☐ some ☐ every ☐ less

Quantifiers: <u>a few</u> and <u>few</u>, <u>a little</u> and <u>little</u>

Use <u>a few</u> with plural count nouns and <u>a little</u> with non-count nouns to mean "some." Use <u>few</u>
with plural count nouns and <u>little</u> with non-count nouns to mean "not many" or "not much."
   A few companies are allowing their employees to dress casually on Fridays. [some companies]
   Few companies are allowing their employees to dress casually on Fridays. [not many companies]
   Employees are showing **a little interest** in this new dress code. [some interest]
   Employees are showing **little interest** in this new dress code. [not much interest]

B Change the underlined quantifiers to <u>a few</u>, <u>few</u>, <u>a little</u>, or <u>little</u>.

a little
   Example: Would you like to listen to ~~some~~ music?

1. We actually eat <u>almost no</u> meat.

2. The newspaper had <u>a bit of</u> information about the concert tonight.

3. There were <u>several</u> new students in my class today.

4. To tell the truth, I've seen <u>hardly any</u> movies in the last month.

5. I enjoy visiting my hometown, but there's <u>not much</u> to do there.

6. If you look in the refrigerator, there should be <u>some</u> eggs.

Quantifiers: using <u>of</u>

Use <u>of</u> (to refer to something specific) when a noun is preceded by a possessive adjective, a possessive noun,
a demonstrative pronoun, or the article <u>the</u>.

most of Jack's co-workers	– **most** co-workers in Italy
several of these companies	– **several** companies
a few of the choices	– **a few** choices
a little of the cake	– **a little** cake
many of those books	– **many** books
any of her friends	– **any** friends
much of the coffee	– **much** coffee
some of his students	– **some** students
each of the classes	– **each** class
one of my cats	– **one** cat
all of our employees	– **all** employees

> **possessive adjectives** my, her, their, etc.
> **possessive nouns** John's, the doctor's
> **demonstrative pronouns** this, that, these, those

> **BE CAREFUL!** In the superlative, do not use <u>of</u> with <u>most</u>.
> DON'T SAY Tokyo is the city with the most ~~of~~ people in Japan.

Using <u>of</u> after <u>all</u> or <u>both</u> is optional, with no change in meaning.
   all of our employees   OR   **all** our employees   NOT   **all** ~~of~~ employees
   both of those choices   OR   **both** those choices   NOT   **both** ~~of~~ choices

> **BE CAREFUL!** <u>Of</u> must be included when using an object pronoun.
> **both of** them   NOT   ~~both them~~

<u>One</u> and <u>each</u> are used with singular nouns only. But <u>one of</u> and <u>each of</u> are used with plural nouns only.
However, the meaning of both expressions is still singular.
   One student   –   **One of** the students
   Each class   –   **Each of** the classes

Some quantifiers must include <u>of</u> when they modify a noun or noun phrase.

a lot of	a majority of
lots of	plenty of
a couple of	a bit of
a number of	a great deal of

C Only one of each pair of sentences is correct. Check the correct sentence and correct the mistake in the other one.

> **Example: a.** ✔ She went with several of her classmates.
>
> **b.** _____ Several ~~of~~ classmates went out for coffee.

1. a. _____ Most of companies in the world are fairly formal.

   b. _____ Most of the companies in the United States have dress-down days.

2. a. _____ All of hot appetizers were delicious.

   b. _____ Everyone tried all of the cold appetizers.

3. a. _____ A lot of my friends have traveled to exotic places.

   b. _____ There are a lot places I'd like to see.

4. a. _____ I read a few of Steinbeck's novels last year.

   b. _____ A few of novels by Steinbeck take place in Mexico.

5. a. _____ Several managers were interviewed, and many them liked the new policy.

   b. _____ Many of the employees we spoke with liked the new policy.

Quantifiers: used without referents

Most quantifiers can be used without the noun they describe as long as the context has been made clear earlier.

A number of people believe there is life on other planets. But **many** don't. [many people]

Grammar for Writing: subject-verb agreement with quantifiers with _of_

In quantifiers with _of_, the verb must agree with the noun that comes after _of_.

Some of **the movie is** in English. – Some of **the movies are** in English.
A lot of **the music was** jazz. – A lot of **the musicians were** young.

In formal English, _none of_ is followed by a singular verb. However, in everyday spoken English, it is common to use it with a plural verb.

Formal: **None of** the students **was** late for class.
Informal: **None of** the students **were** late for class.

> **BE CAREFUL!** The quantifiers one of, each of, and every one of are always followed by a plural noun, but they always take a singular verb.
> One of the students likes rap music.

D Choose the verb that agrees with each subject.

  1. Every one of these choices (sound / sounds) terrific!

  2. One of the teachers (was / were) going to stay after class.

  3. A lot of the problem (is / are) that no one wants to work so hard.

  4. Each of the employees (want / wants) to work overtime.

  5. Half of the city (was / were) flooded in the storm.

  6. None of the players (is coming / are coming) to the game.

  7. Only 8 percent of their workers prefer shorter work weeks, while at least 90 percent (don't / doesn't).

Unit 5

Conjunctions with so, too, neither, or not either

Use **and so** or **and . . . too** to join affirmative statements that are similar.
> Spitting on the street is offensive, **and so** is littering.
> OR Spitting on the street is offensive, **and** littering is **too**.

Use **neither** or **not either** to join negative statements that are similar.
> Spitting on the street doesn't bother me, **and neither** does littering.
> Spitting on the street doesn't bother me, **and** littering doesn't **either**.

If the first clause uses the verb **be**, an auxiliary verb, or a modal, use the same structure in the second clause.
> Tokyo **is** a huge city, and so **is** São Paulo.
> New York **doesn't** have a lot of industry, and neither **does** London.
> Mexico City **has** grown a lot, and so **has** Los Angeles.
> Nancy **can't** tolerate loud radios, and neither **can** Tom.

If the first clause does not include the verb **be**, an auxiliary verb, or a modal, use a form of **do**.
> John **thinks** graffiti is a big problem, and so **does** Helen.

> **BE CAREFUL!** Use a negative with **either** and an affirmative with **neither**.
> . . . and **neither** does littering.
> NOT . . . and neither doesn't littering.
> . . . and littering **doesn't either**.
> NOT . . . and littering does either.

> **BE CAREFUL!** Notice the subject-verb order.
> . . . and so **is** littering.
> . . . and **littering is** too.
> . . . and neither **does** littering.
> . . . and **littering doesn't** either.

> **BE CAREFUL!** With **so** and **neither**, the verb (or auxiliary verb) goes before the subject.
> Nancy can't stand loud boom boxes, and neither **can** Tom.
> NOT . . . neither Tom can.
> Tokyo is a huge city, and so **is São Paulo**.
> NOT . . . and so São Paulo is.

A Find and underline the nine errors. On a separate sheet of paper, write each sentence correctly.

New York is one of the most famous cities in the world, and so does London. While these two cities differ in many ways, they also share a number of characteristics. Here's a quick comparison:

- If you're looking for peace and quiet, New York is not the place to be, and neither London is. They are both exciting and noisy places. If you're not used to it, New York's traffic can be deafening at times, and so does London's.
- The best way to get around in both cities is the subway (or the Tube in London). New York's subway system is quite old and elaborate, and is London's too.

- If you're looking for first-rate entertainment, New York is filled with theaters, and so London does.
- Hungry? London's restaurants feature exciting dishes from around the world, and New York's are too.
- Both cities offer a huge choice of museums to visit. The museums in New York can't possibly be seen in a day, and either London's can't.
- New York offers some of the world's most famous tourist sites—for example, the Statue of Liberty and the Empire State Building—and so is London, with Buckingham Palace and the Millennium Wheel.

It's clear that New York shouldn't be missed, and neither London shouldn't!

B On a separate sheet of paper, rewrite each statement, using the word in parentheses. Make any necessary changes in verbs or possessive adjectives.

Example: Both Vilnius and Riga have large historic districts. (so)

Vilnius has a large historic district, and so does Riga.

1. Both Bangkok and São Paulo face many problems caused by too much traffic. (so)
2. Both Athens and Barcelona have hosted the Olympic Games in the past. (too)
3. Vancouver and Taipei don't ever get very cold. (neither)
4. Mexico City and Tokyo won't experience a decrease in their populations any time soon. (not either)
5. Both Hong Kong and Rio de Janeiro are famous for their physical beauty. (so)
6. Prague and Krakow attract people who like great architecture. (too)
7. The Prado Museum in Madrid and the Louvre in Paris shouldn't be missed. (neither)
8. Tokyo and Mexico City haven't lost their places among the world's largest cities yet. (not either)

Unit 7

Vowel sounds /i/ and /ɪ/

The sound /i/ is longer and is formed by tensing the tongue.
The sound /ɪ/ is shorter and formed with the tongue relaxed.

/i/	/ɪ/
leave	live
team	Tim
feel	fill
steal	still
feet	fit

The vowel sound /ɪ/ also appears frequently in unstressed syllables.

— •   — •   — • •   — •   — •
places   market   artisan   minute   women

The vowel sounds /i/ and /ɪ/ are represented in spelling in a number of ways.

/i/	/ɪ/
steal	blimp
steep	syllable
people	busy
handy	building
believe	women
receive	pretty
boutique	been
key	give

A 🎧 5:16 Listen and practice.

1. leave   live
2. team   Tim
3. feel   fill
4. steal   still
5. feet   fit

B 🎧 5:17 Listen and practice.

1. places   2. market   3. artisan   4. minute   5. women

C 🎧 5:18 Listen to each pair of words. Circle if they are the <u>same</u> or <u>different</u>.

1. same   different   5. same   different
2. same   different   6. same   different
3. same   different   7. same   different
4. same   different   8. same   different

D 🎧 5:19 Listen and check which sound you hear in the stressed syllable.

	/i/ /ɪ/		/i/ /ɪ/		/i/ /ɪ/
1. ☐ ☐		6. ☐ ☐		11. ☐ ☐	
2. ☐ ☐		7. ☐ ☐		12. ☐ ☐	
3. ☐ ☐		8. ☐ ☐		13. ☐ ☐	
4. ☐ ☐		9. ☐ ☐		14. ☐ ☐	
5. ☐ ☐		10. ☐ ☐			

🎧 5:19 Now listen again and practice.

Unit 8

Stress placement: prefixes and suffixes

Stress placement does not change when most prefixes and suffixes are added to a word.

important   unimportant   importance   importantly

obedient   obedience   disobedience   obediently

happy   unhappy   happiness   happily

However, adding the suffixes -ion, -ic, -ity, -ical, and -ian generally shifts stress to the syllable before the suffix.

educate   →   education

photograph   →   photographic

dependable   →   dependability

politics   →   political

music   →   musician

Some nouns and verbs have the same spelling. When the word is a noun, the stress is on the first syllable. When the word is a verb the stress is on the second syllable.

nouns	verbs
rebel	rebel
protest	protest
present	present
object	object
progress	progress

Other words in this category
- conduct
- conflict
- contrast
- convert
- permit
- record
- survey
- suspect

A 🎧 5:20 Listen and practice.

1. important   unimportant   importance   importantly
2. obedient   obedience   disobedience   obediently
3. happy   unhappy   happiness   happily

B 🎧 5:21 Listen and practice.

1. educate   education
2. photograph   photographic
3. dependable   dependability
4. politics   political
5. music   musician

C Look at the stressed syllable of each word in Column A. According to the rules given in the chart on page P7, mark the stressed syllable of each word in Column B.

A	B
1. fa <u>mil</u> iar	fa mil iar i ty
2. e <u>mo</u> tion al	e mo tion al ly
3. <u>reg</u> u late	reg u la tion
4. ap <u>pre</u> ci a tive	ap pre cia tive ly
5. <u>sym</u> pa thy	sym pa thet ic
6. hy <u>poth</u> e size	hy po thet i cal
7. <u>beau</u> ty	beau ti fy
8. <u>his</u> to ry	his tor i cal
9. ma <u>te</u> ri al ist	ma te ri al is tic
10. <u>pol</u> i tics	pol i ti cian

5:22
🎧 Now practice reading each word aloud and listen to check.*

D 5:23 🎧 Listen and practice.

nouns	verbs
1. rebel	rebel
2. protest	protest
3. present	present
4. object	object
5. progress	progress

E Circle the syllable you think will be stressed in each blue word.

1. A summer fishing **permit permits** you to fish all you want.
2. The **protest** was organized to **protest** government spending.
3. All the employees were **surveyed** so the results of the **survey** would be useful.
4. The **contrast** between them now is not great compared to how much they **contrast** at other times of the year.
5. We strongly **object** to the decision to sell art **objects** outside the museum.

5:24
🎧 Now practice reading each sentence aloud, paying attention to words that are both nouns and verbs. Listen to check.*

Unit 9

Reduction and linking in perfect modals in the passive voice

In perfect modals in the passive voice, the modal and the auxiliary verbs <u>have been</u> are said together as one unit. Note that stress falls on the modal and the main verb. In everyday speech, the /h/ sound in the auxilliary <u>have</u> is dropped and /æ/ is reduced to /ə/.

/'kʊdəvbɪn/
They **COULD have been KILLED**.

/'maɪtəvbɪn/
They **MIGHT have been LOST**.

/'məstəvbɪn/
They **MUST have been MOVED**.

/'meɪyəvbɪn/
They **MAY have been DISCOVERED**.

With <u>had to</u>, stress <u>had</u> and the main verb. Say <u>had to</u> and <u>have been</u> as one unit.

/'hætuəvbɪn/
They **HAD to have been STOLEN**.

In negative perfect modals, stress falls on the modal, the word <u>not</u>, and the main verb. In everyday speech, <u>not</u> and the auxiliary verbs <u>have been</u> are generally said as one unit.

/'natəvbɪn/
They **MIGHT NOT have been LOST**.
They **MUST NOT have been MOVED**.

A 🎧 5:25 Listen and practice.

1. They could have been killed.
2. They might have been lost.
3. They must have been moved.
4. They may have been discovered.
5. They had to have been stolen.
6. They might not have been lost.
7. They must not have been moved.

B Underline where you think the words should be linked and which sounds should be reduced.

1. The dinosaurs may have been killed by a meteor.
2. The trees could have been destroyed by a fire.
3. The gold figures may not have been lost.
4. The stone balls must have been moved using animals.
5. The drawings must not have been discovered until later.
6. The crater had to have been caused by a meteorite.
7. The trees couldn't have been burned in a fire.

🎧 5:26 Now practice reading each sentence aloud, paying attention to reductions. Listen to check.*

Unit 10

Vowel sounds /eɪ/, /ɛ/, /æ/, and /ʌ/

The sound /eɪ/ is longer and is formed by tensing the tongue with the lips spread.
The sounds /ɛ/, /æ/, and /ʌ/ are shorter and are formed with the tongue relaxed.
Say /eɪ/ and /ɛ/ with the lips spread wide. Say /æ/ with the lips spread slightly and the
mouth slightly open. Say /ʌ/ with the tongue and jaw completely relaxed.

Mouth positions for vowels	
tongue tensed (long)	/eɪ/
tongue relaxed (short)	/ɛ/, /æ/, /ʌ/
lips spread	/eɪ/, /ɛ/, /æ/
jaw relaxed	/ʌ/

/eɪ/	/ɛ/	/æ/	/ʌ/
pain	pen	pan	pun
Dane	den	Dan	done
mate	met	mat	mutt
bait	bet	bat	but

The vowel sounds /eɪ/, /ɛ/, /æ/, and /ʌ/ may
be represented by these spellings.

/eɪ/	/ɛ/	/æ/	/ʌ/
pay	get	catch	jumping
weigh	sweat	have	nothing
shape	says	laugh	touch
wait	said	half	does
table	friend	guarantee	blood
great	guest	relax	what

A 🎧 5:27 Listen and practice.

1. pain   pen   pan   pun
2. Dane   den   Dan   done
3. mate   met   mat   mutt
4. bait   bet   bat   but

B 🎧 5:28 Listen to each word and place it in the correct column.

edge   games   enough   can't   bungee   rafting   nothing   chance   sweat   wait   scare

/eɪ/	/ɛ/	/æ/	/ʌ/

🎧 5:28 Now practice reading each word aloud and listen again to check.*

C 🎧 5:29 Listen to each sentence and circle the word you hear.

1. Give the money to the (men / man).
2. I think it's (Dan / done).
3. What is that (rag / rug) made of?
4. Do you need this (pen / pan)?
5. He's a perfect (mutt / mate).
6. My (date / debt) is causing me trouble.
7. Could you take that (bug / bag) off the counter?
8. Please put a bandage on the (cut / cat).

Now practice reading the sentences both ways.